PHYSICIANS
AND THEIR IMAGES

First published in Great Britain in 2018 by Little, Brown

Unless otherwise indicated, all images are from the RCP collections and all photography is by Mike Fear.

Designed by Emil Dacanay and Sian Rance, D.R. ink

A CIP catalogue record for this book is available from the British Library.

ISBN 978-1-4087-0636-7

Printed in China

COVER: Artist unknown, *William Harvey*, n.d., 133.9 x 108.5.
PAGE 1: William Miller, after an unknown artist, *Thomas Linacre*, 1810, 48.3 x 36.8.
OPPOSITE: Artist unknown, *Theodore Turquet de Mayerne*, n.d., 127 x 90.1.

500
REFLECTIONS
ON THE RCP
1518-2018

PHYSICIANS
AND THEIR IMAGES

Ludmilla Jordanova

Royal College
of Physicians

Taken together, the portraits and architecture around the central staircase speak to the College's identity; they suggest its long history blends with modern values.

FOREWORD

The Royal College of Physicians was founded, by Royal Charter, in 1518 by King Henry VIII. Few professional organisations have been in continuous existence for so long, and over its five-hundred-year history the College has been at the centre of many aspects of medical life. Its principal purpose is to promote the highest standards of medical practice in order to improve health and healthcare, and its varied work in the field is held in high regard. Currently, the College has over thirty thousand members and fellows worldwide. Over the years it has also accumulated a distinguished library, extensive archives and a collection of portraits and other treasures, and has been housed in a number of notable buildings. As part of its quincentennial commemoration, a series of ten books has been commissioned. Each book features fifty reflections, thereby making a total of five hundred, intended to be a meditation on, and an exploration of, aspects of the College's work and its collections over its five-hundred-year history.

This eighth volume in the series is a fascinating exploration of medical portraits, and their meanings and signification. It is based on the superb archives and collections of the Royal College of Physicians and the book is an exposition, from various perspectives, of the portraits and of their contexts. It is a scholarly work by a renowned figure in the field, Ludmilla Jordanova, who is Professor of History and Visual Culture and Director of the Centre for Visual Arts and Culture at Durham University. There is no person better equipped to have taken on the task of writing this book.

The College's grateful thanks are also offered to all who have helped in the production of this book, and especially to Julie Beckwith, Head of the Library at the College, who has assisted in finding the images and arranging their photography. Special thanks too are due to Professor Linda Luxon, who has been intimately involved in the production of the volume, to the staff in the medical publishing department, led by Natalie Wilder, and to our publisher.

Simon Shorvon -

**Simon Shorvon, Harveian Librarian 2012–16, Royal College of Physicians
Series Editor**

CONTENTS

THE FIFTY FEATURED PORTRAITS

ACKNOWLEDGEMENTS

My greatest debt is to the officers and staff of the College, with whom it has been a privilege and a pleasure to work. I thank them most warmly for the opportunity to engage with the collections. I have also drawn on the resources of the National Portrait Gallery in London, especially the Heinz Archive; the National Library of Scotland; the library and archives of Emmanuel College, Cambridge; Cambridge University Library; and the libraries of Durham University. Members of staff at all these institutions have been extremely helpful. I give warm thanks to Helen Carron, Finola Finn, Jeff Hughes, Lauren Kassell, Laurence Klein, Tristan Lake, Howard Nelson and Simon Schaffer for their help, and to the owner of the painting of Elizabeth Garrett Anderson by John Singer Sargent for permission to reproduce it here. My family, close friends and colleagues have been wonderfully supportive. At the College I have benefited especially from the generous advice and assistance of Julie Beckwith, Simon Shorvon, Natalie Wilder and Beth Wilkey.

LJJ

Bewlie and Durham

Autumn 2016

OPPOSITE: Thomas Lawrence, *Henry Halford*, c. 1825–30, 142.2 x 111.8.

PREFACE

Portraits are complex deposits of relationships: between artists and sitters, between collectors and their possessions, between institutions and their members, between patrons, friends, clients and viewers. They could not exist without framers, suppliers of materials and conservators, who provide an infrastructure for artists and owners, as galleries and auction houses do for audiences and collectors.

Thus an intricate nexus of relationships gives rise to this important art form. In *Physicians and Their Images* I explore some of these relationships for a single institution, using its collections, archives and other available evidence, including biographies, the writings of some of the key players and materials from other institutions, such as the National Portrait Gallery in London. There is much of value to draw upon, especially the printed catalogues of the portraits and other College publications.

I have sought to do justice to a distinctive collection and to suggest how it is possible to approach portraiture, which is arguably one of the most significant artistic genres. Portraits are deemed capable of bringing human beings to the minds of their fellows using inert materials. This drive to capture something of the existence of another person has been strong in many contexts, especially in the English-speaking world. Institutional collections are especially revealing because they express a sense of continuity over long periods of time. They link individuals to the history of their occupation. In the case of the Royal College of Physicians in London, the story goes back to ancient times, since classical figures such as Hippocrates were revered, read and debated there for centuries. More immediately, we are considering continuities over the last five hundred years, which portraits help to symbolise. They speak to an institutional past of half a millennium and serve as enduring visible reminders both of corporate life and of specific individuals.

The Royal College of Physicians possesses a strong sense of its own history, which portraits help to create and sustain. They assist in building and shoring up the reputation of distinguished doctors by acting as a focal point for remembering their achievements. It is striking how many medical practitioners have a well-developed interest in the past of their field. When brought together in the College, fellows and members express their historical awareness in a number of mutually reinforcing ways: by commemorating illustrious predecessors in dinners and speeches; naming rooms after them; collecting artefacts connected to them; writing and reading obituaries, memoirs and histories; and by acquiring, commenting on and reproducing portraits. Portraits take many forms, including prints, photographs, frontispieces and drawings; they can be used to shape an understanding of the medical past in journals, books, magazines, freestanding images and digital products. By

HIPPOCRATES.
Taken from a Gem in the possession of J. Tassie Esq.r in Leicester Square.
London, Published Oct.r 11, 1809, by J. Wilkes.

ABOVE: J. Chapman, *Hippocrates. Taken from a Gem in the possession of J. Tassie Esq in Leicester Square*, 1809, stipple engraving, 18.5 x 12.8.
Hippocrates has been portrayed innumerable times, while his writings remained of deep interest to at least some medical practitioners well into the nineteenth century. James Tassie was a successful gem engraver and modeller who made many small medallion heads of famous individuals. In the little scene below a semi-recumbent man is being tended, presumably by Hippocrates, while Old Father Time holds an hourglass and a scythe.
OPPOSITE: The Censors' Room is the historical heart of the College. The panelling was brought from earlier buildings and it is dense with portraits.

examining the diverse uses of portraits, it becomes possible to appreciate how figures, including those from a distant past, remain, as it were, alive in the minds of their successors, while recently commissioned works will, it is anticipated, sustain the memories of future generations of physicians.

This book contains my selection of fifty items from the College's collections. In order to help make sense of these works, there are additional illustrations which serve as context for the former and to extend readers' understanding of the collection and of portraiture as a genre. The essential information – the names of maker and sitter, the date of production, medium and size, if known – is given in the caption. Unless otherwise stated, all works are owned by the College and are oil on canvas. Measurements are given in centimetres with height before width. The index gives the dates of birth and death of individuals and includes organisations. For the sake of economy, I have generally omitted people's titles. It has not been possible to illustrate all the portraits mentioned, but simple internet searches should provide an image quickly.

My selection is designed to reveal the breadth and depth of the collection, to include women as well as men, to take the quality of work into account, and to illustrate the possibilities of different media. Balancing these goals has not been easy and inevitably personal preference has played a part. I have not sought to select the 'best' works, however that may be defined, but to focus on portraits that shed light on recurrent themes, which include the elaborate ties of kinship and friendship that characterise medical life, the close interest that many physicians have taken in both collecting and the history of their occupation, and forms of patronage. Medicine is a domain with intimate links to art and literature; indeed, it is a field that is itself a form of culture. It is worth remembering that the College, although based in London, has forged links with practitioners in many parts of the British Isles and wider afield.

Notes and bibliography are presented economically and placed at the end. Standard biographical sources, such as William Munk's *The Roll of the Royal College of Physicians* and the *Oxford Dictionary of National Biography*, and the printed catalogues of portraits, are not included in the notes. In the selection of portraits, there is a weighting towards works in oil. The College has relatively small collections of three-dimensional works, drawings and watercolours, but a substantial number of prints, of which I have been able to include just a tiny fraction here. Photography is mentioned only in passing. Prints played a central role in circulating portraits of physicians to wider audiences than their originals could reach in the pre-photographic era. While it was common to make copies of some oil paintings, derivative prints were exceptionally important. Magazines and newspapers, as well as satirical publications, have also been significant. Sadly, it has proved impossible to do justice to this aspect of *Physicians and Their Images* here. I hope that what follows reveals the richness of the College's collections and some of the ways in which they can be approached so as to deepen our understanding of the organisation and its history, and of portraiture as a genre.

Felix Szczesny Kwarta, *Albert Schweitzer*, 1953, 89.5 x 71.1.
Schweitzer was famous for his medical work in Africa as well as for his organ-playing and theological writings.
He received the Nobel Peace Prize in 1952 and was honoured in the UK with the Order of Merit in 1955.
Schweitzer was much represented; indeed, he was a celebrity. His portrait serves as a reminder of networks of
association between medical professionals across the world. The Polish artist was interned in Bergen-Belsen
and escaped to England, where he spent the rest of his life.

ABOVE: Halford's portrait by Lawrence is in the centre of a large, dramatic hang on the first floor of the building. The painting was bequeathed by his grandson. The College also owns a bust by Chantrey of its longest-serving President.
OPPOSITE: Merlyn Evans, *Robert Platt*, 1963, 125.7 x 100.3, frame 157 x 131.8.
Platt was President between 1957 and 1962, a crucial time in the College's history when he was deeply involved in commissioning Denys Lasdun to design and erect the current building. Platt's autobiography, *Private and Controversial*, published in 1972, discusses the College.

SETTING THE SCENE

Anyone walking into the Royal College of Physicians, a celebrated modern building on the edge of Regent's Park, must be struck by the profusion of portraits displayed there. In the entrance hall an eighteenth-century bust of William Harvey, arguably the most famous fellow, is embedded in the wall. On the ground floor hang large canvases, mostly from the seventeenth and eighteenth centuries, and so it is throughout the building that paintings and busts abound. When designing the building Denys Lasdun paid careful attention to the culture, practices and values of his patrons, mentioning portraits early on in his notes. As Robert Platt, the President at the time, put it, 'Lasdun took endless care in studying the functions, customs and ceremonies of the college and examining also its portraits and other possessions…'[1] The very fabric of this stunning building is in harmony with the oil paintings and sculptures it contains. Evidently, portraits remain integral to College life.

The phrase *Physicians and Their Images* refers to both those that they own and those that depict them. There is a further meaning of 'image' – the impression that an individual or group conveys to others as well as prevailing assumptions about them.[2] Medical practitioners have long been concerned with their status and the esteem in which they are held by other parties, especially patients, elites and governments. Yet the image of doctors in the wider world is not within their control; they can only deploy all the means at their disposal to manage it. Hence visual and verbal rhetoric are integral to presenting images of physicians both within peer groups and to lay audiences. There are complicated dynamics here, and portraits certainly play their part.

It is worth reflecting on the peculiar vulnerability of the medical profession, which makes a concern with image in its broadest sense an important theme. Doctors' basic material is the human body in all its states and hence they consider matters that are intimate and emotionally charged, touching patients' fundamental qualities, whether they carry out physical examinations or not. They may well be the harbingers of death. In most historical situations, as today, a wide range of therapies and practitioners is available – patients make choices, often they pay and inevitably they judge. The status of medical knowledge, and of those who profess it, is necessarily carefully crafted. These processes become evident when the intellectual reputation of key figures is discussed. One familiar trope associated physicians with learning rather than the manual skills of surgeons, doing so in contexts where the head took precedence over the hand. These stereotypes are reductive, but this does not lessen their grip on the imagination.[3] We can pick up on such phenomena through the language used in biographies, memoirs and obituaries and the visual idioms deployed in portraits.

The key element in a 'portrait' is the representation, in any medium, of a specific human being, who has a name even if it has been lost, and in such a way that they could, somehow, be recognised.

The term 'portrait' needs to be defined. I consider images of classical figures, such as Hippocrates and Galen, to be 'portraits' in that those who made them believed they were depicting an actual named person and providing an account of their features as best they could, given the available evidence. Thus the key element in a 'portrait' is the representation, in any medium, of a specific human being, who has a name even if it has been lost, and in such a way that they could, somehow, be recognised. Avant-garde portraits – Picasso's cubist ones, for example – might be seen as stretching the point about recognisability, but works commissioned by professional bodies tend to be more conventional and those in the Royal College of Physicians are no exception.[4] An unusual work is the portrait of Richard Thompson by Diarmuid Kelley, in which the sitter is nonetheless fully recognisable and the overall approach is strongly naturalistic, while parts of the canvas remain unpainted. 'Portrait' generally implies some degree of formality, if only through the process of sitting for the artist, together with some kind of transaction – contract, payment and transfer of rights, for example. Thus Annigoni's formal portrait of Lord Moran may be contrasted with the informal snaps in the Wellcome Trust's collection, which depict him on holiday; in one he is even wearing what looks like a tea towel on his head. The latter are not 'portraits'.

Not all portraits were done from life; sometimes it is difficult to know what the processes involved were. Direct evidence from the sitters' books kept by artists, where they record the dates of sittings and sometimes other information about the commission, is thus especially valuable. In many cases, painters and their clients moved in the same circles, hence their encounters took place in contexts where much was known about each other's personalities and lives. There is an important element of trust at work here. Sitters in particular trust that artists will choose appropriate visual idioms when depicting them. After all, artists are highly skilled agents, who draw

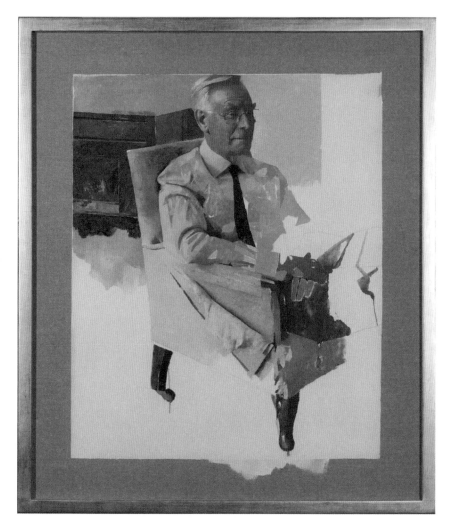

Diarmuid Kelley, *Richard Thompson*, 2015, in frame 117 x 102. The gold frame is 3cm wide.

on their knowledge and experience to create a likeness. I am not referring to simple flattery here, but to the concern that occupations and institutions present images that are appropriate, and this requires portrait painters to grasp their sitters' social, economic and political situations. It is hardly surprising, then, that 'portrait' can be a vivid metaphor for a faithful account, be it of a period, an occupation, a building or a country. Nor should it be a surprise that portraits engender conversations – indeed, that is one of their social functions. They invite viewers to remember, to ask questions, to make comparisons, to muse on lives and to articulate feelings. Precisely which conversations arise in any given instance depends, at least in part, on the physical

Allan Wyon, *Medal in Honour of Walter Moxon*, gold, 1939, 6.4cm diameter.
Medals, and hence the portraits upon them, convey authority and achievement. Here Walter Moxon is
honoured; he became a fellow in 1868 and was a noted anatomist. The medal was first awarded in 1891, five
years after Moxon's death, and is given triennially. It recognises observation and research in clinical medicine.
This one was presented to the College by Sir Arthur Hurst, who had received it in 1939; his name is engraved
on the rim. In giving material form to past achievements, medals bind the recipient to the person depicted and
to their achievements, and both of them to the institution, shown on the reverse.

properties of the likeness in question. One of the most significant of these is scale.
There are two aspects of scale to consider. The first is the dimensions of the depiction
in relation to the human body. Can it be held in the hand or worn about the person?
How far away need the viewer stand in order to appreciate the whole work? In the
case of a three-dimensional portrait, we must consider whether it was designed to be
seen from all sides. And in every case the position in which it is displayed is crucial.
Thus architectural settings for portraits are integral to viewers' experiences, which are
shaped by colour and texture as well as scale.

Portraits also possess what we can think of as internal scale. Viewers pick up,
almost without being aware of doing so, how much of the subject's body is depicted,
and in how much detail, and where they are placed in the visual field in the case
of two-dimensional works. In some portraits elaborate accoutrements, drapery and
background scenes provide further ways of locating and experiencing the figure.
In others no further visual cues are given. Compare, for example, the depictions of
William Cadogan and Edward Archer by the same artist (pages 20–21), and then both
of them with the medals and miniatures in this volume.

While portraits can be made in any medium, there is a hierarchy of media, just as there was a hierarchy of artistic genres, in which portraiture came significantly below the painting of historical and biblical scenes. Since the advent of oil paints as a widely used medium in the sixteenth century, they became, along with marble and bronze, prestigious media for portraiture. Some large works in oil have been termed 'swagger portraits', depicting their subjects in the grand manner associated with rulers and elites. The College possesses some such portraits, Thomas Lawrence's painting of Sir Henry Halford (c. 1825–30), for example (see page 9). There are a number of interconnected issues here. One is certainly cost. We can contrast the depiction of Halford with the same artist's painting of Edward Jenner, also in the College's collections. This consists of a head of no special merit, costing considerably less than a full-length portrait. The scale of a portrait has immediate implications for the ways in which it can be displayed. How much of the sitter's body is shown is closely connected to the claims about status a picture contains. This is why Hogarth's 1740 full-length portrait of the founder of the Foundling Hospital, Thomas Coram, makes such a radical statement in depicting the sea captain seated on a dais, with a distant view of the sea, a column and tumbling fabric behind him. It hangs next to Allan Ramsay's monumental portrait of Richard Mead as the learned physician and collector.[5] Comparable works in the College include Jonathan Richardson's portrait of Richard Hale, the portrait of John Radcliffe from Kneller's studio, and Sir William Browne (1767) by Thomas Hudson, Hogarth's teacher.

ABOVE: Allan Ramsay, *Richard Mead*, 1747, 262.2 x 144.8, Thomas Coram Foundation. Mead is credited with helping Ramsay get established when he first moved to London from Scotland in 1732. © Coram in the care of the Foundling Museum.

How much of the sitter's body is shown is closely connected to the claims about status a picture contains.

LEFT ABOVE: R. W. Dickinson after Robert Edge Pine, *William Cadogan*, mezzotint, 1772, 38.5 x 28.5.

This fine mezzotint is probably derived from Pine's painting, given to the College in 1828. Mezzotints, with their velvety tones, were used to convey the feel of oil paintings.

Cadogan became a Governor of the London Foundling Hospital in 1747 and its physician six years later. His *Essay on Nursing*, 1748, was inspired by his association with this institution, which possessed a significant art collection that could be seen by the public. His influential essay gave child-rearing advice.

LEFT BELOW: Jonathan Richardson, *Richard Hale*, n.d., 125.4 x 101.5.

Hale's portrait emphasises his doctor's robe and uses background drapery to add to the effect. Richardson was an important figure in the English art world, a writer about art as well as a successful portrait painter.

He depicted Richard Mead, Hans Sloane and William Cheselden and was a friend of Thomas Birch, who frequented Mead's dining club. Hale held a number of hospital posts and amassed a considerable fortune. He was active in the College, giving the Harveian Oration in 1724.

OPPOSITE: Robert Edge Pine, *Edward Archer*, 1782, 243.8 x 152.4.

Archer's elegant gesture invites viewers to pay attention to the building, presumably the Smallpox Hospital, where he had worked since 1747 and where, at his express wish, he died in 1789. Possessed of private means, he owned a fine library. The painting portrays an institution as well as a person in a grand interior.

John Collier, *William Munk*, 1898, 90.8 x 71.1.
Munk served as Harveian Librarian from 1857 until his death in 1898. While he is best known for writing about the lives of fellows and licentiates of the College, he also published a book on euthanasia in 1887. His 1895 *Life of Sir Henry Halford* shows him to be a sensitive historian who considered that, since his subject had been dead for more than fifty years, he could now be studied. He saw that Halford could shed light on 'the social history of his time' and, as a historian, he ought to 'place [him]self *in* the period of which [he is] speaking and *out* of the period in which [he is] actually writing'. (His emphasis.)

Copies were made from oil paintings, called a replica if done by the original artist, and derivative prints were readily produced if there was thought to be a market for them. Uniqueness, so highly prized in the present day, was not the only criterion of value. John Collier, the artist who portrayed William Munk, also depicted Thomas Henry Huxley, Charles Darwin and other leading figures in the worlds of science and medicine: he painted replicas in many cases.

Louis-François Roubiliac, *Richard Mead*, n.d., 69.9 high.
Askew presented this classicising bust to the College in 1756, two years after Mead's death.

Three-dimensional portraits also invite our attention, whether in the form of medals and medallions or statues and busts. Again, diverse materials have been used – metals, marble, terracotta, plaster, wax and ceramic – with marble and metal conveying connotations of prestige. The rich interplay between public monuments, classical sculpture and three-dimensional portraits is significant, especially when sitters are shown in attire reminiscent of classical dress, as in Roubiliac's bust of Mead presented to the College by Mead's friend Anthony Askew. Since the sculptor

In each portrait, medium and scale, as well as composition and palette, hint at the settings and audiences for which they were originally designed.

was a major figure in Britain's art scene, some of the prestige derived from his previous work and fame as well as from the classical reference, the use of marble and the sitter's reputation as scholar, philanthropist, collector and physician.[6]

Other media, such as pastel, watercolour, pen, charcoal and pencil, are also worth noting. William Haines' depiction of William Macmichael, small in size and in delicate hues, gives viewers a sense of easy familiarity with the sitter. The drawings of George Burrows and Charles Mansfield Clarke, with their light touch and mere hint of colour, are quite unlike a highly finished oil painting. In each portrait, medium and scale, as well as composition and palette, hint at the settings and audiences for which they were originally designed, generally markedly different from their current location in a modernist building, and their public audience.

TOP LEFT: William Haines, *William Macmichael*, watercolours on paper, 1823, 30.3 x 24.8.
Macmichael had successfully published an account of his travels in Greece, Russia, Bulgaria, Turkey and Palestine before he wrote *The Gold-headed Cane*. His journeys were supported by funds left by John Radcliffe. Macmichael was well connected and helped by the patronage of Sir Henry Halford. He held royal appointments, was active in the College and a fellow of the Royal Society. He compiled *Lives of British Physicians*, first published in 1830, a good example of the popularity of biographies, accompanied by portraits, in affordable formats.
TOP CENTRE: George Richmond, *George Burrows*, red and black chalks on paper, n.d., 61 x 45.
Richmond painted Burrows in 1871, the year he became President of the College, wearing his robes, seated and holding a book. This undated drawing by Richmond was presumably associated with the painting. The son of a physician, Burrows married a daughter of John Abernethy, the surgeon. He was also active on the General Medical Council and in the British Medical Association. Burrows was one of Queen Victoria's physicians and a fellow of the Royal Society, and was made a baronet in 1874.
TOP RIGHT: Joseph Slater, *Charles Mansfield Clarke*, 1822, red and black chalks on paper, 29.9 x 23.8.
Compared with the painting of Clarke, made around 1832, this drawing is intimate and approachable. Francis Chantrey also drew and sculpted Clarke.

BELOW: Artist unknown, *Samuel Gee and Edith Gee*, watercolours on ivory, n.d., each portrait 7.1 diameter, case 12.5 x 21.6 when open.

Samuel Gee became a fellow of the College in 1870, was a successful practitioner and active in the College, and wrote *Auscultation and Percussion* (1870). Little is known about the circumstances under which these miniatures were produced. One of Samuel's daughters and his wife predeceased him, so perhaps these images show a special attachment between father and daughter as the surviving members of the family. Edith bequeathed them to the College. Before her death she had given another portrait of her father to the College.

ABOVE: Samuel Lane, *Charles Mansfield Clarke*, 1832, 127 x 99.1.
Clarke came from a medical family and was a successful accoucheur. This picture, given to the College by a descendant, uses many familiar devices for suggesting a serious, well-educated man, including resting his head on his hand, a finger marking his place in a book and the papers on the table covered with a patterned cloth. Clarke was physician to Queen Adelaide and was made a baronet in 1831.

EDITH THYRA GEE

Dᴿ SAMUEL GEE

The majority of the works in the College's collections honour people who were medical practitioners, mostly those who held high office in the organisation. These portraits have been acquired through purchase, donation and commission. When known, their provenance provides valuable clues to their significance and to the nature of medical lives. Families play a central role, with portraits of relations also joining the collections. For instance, there are the matching miniatures of the physician Samuel Gee and his daughter Edith, and depictions of members of the Baillie family, relations of William and John Hunter. Images of royal patrons are also present.

ABOVE: Artist unknown, *Theodore Turquet de Mayerne*, n.d., 127 x 90.1.
Mayerne, who was born in Geneva, became a prominent figure at the English court. He first spent time in England in 1606, returning for a longer spell in 1610. A number of representations of him exist, including a portrait by Rubens, in Mead's collection. Mayerne had a strong interest in the visual arts, writing about artistic techniques and pigments.
TOP RIGHT: Joshua Reynolds, *William Pitcairn*, 1777, 76.2 x 63.5.
Pitcairn served ten years as President of the College; during that time he was painted by one of the leading artists of the day. Reynolds was President of the Royal Academy and friendly with numerous writers, collectors and intellectuals, many of whom he painted. Five sittings were noted by Reynolds, who was paid thirty-five guineas for the portrait, which was bequeathed to the College by the widow of Pitcairn's nephew.
BOTTOM RIGHT: James McArdell after Joshua Reynolds, *Charles Lucas*, mezzotint, 1755–65, 32.6 x 22.5.
Reynolds painted Lucas, a well-known Irish patriot, in 1755. The title of his Leyden thesis, awarded in 1752, is shown in the picture. He became a licentiate of the College in 1759.

Most portraits depict men, although since women have played a role in the medical professions and specifically in the College, their likenesses have entered the collection. Well-established idioms for depicting men could not necessarily be applied to women, hence their portraits – the earliest in the collection dates from 1955, although earlier images of female relatives exist – are relevant for our understanding of gender. Many works are by makers well known in their own times, even if some names are less familiar today. Considering the wider *oeuvres* of artists helps us to set likenesses of medical professionals in a broad context. Joshua Reynolds, for instance, was skilled at painting middle-class men, including scholars, writers, musicians and medical practitioners.[7]

Power, wealth and royal connections sometimes underpinned a high medical reputation and prompted the production of a likeness.

Artist unknown, after Hans Holbein, *John Chambre*, oil on panel, n.d., 27.9 x 22.9

Chambre was a cleric as well as one of the physicians named in the College's founding charter. Like Harvey he studied at Padua and was a royal physician. His career in the church was successful, and he spent nineteen years as Warden of Merton College, Oxford. The open book makes clear his association with anatomy, while the skull and hourglass are familiar *memento mori*.

LEFT: William Daniell after George Dance, *John Moore*, soft ground etching, 1808, 27.8 x 8.6.
Moore's main reputation was as a writer and many prints of him exist. He originally trained as a surgeon, practising as a physician later on, but was never a fellow of the College.
The artist, George Dance, was a well-known architect who produced numerous profile portraits, including of scientific and medical figures, which could be made into prints. Many of these were by William Daniell, who was a landscape painter as well as an engraver.
RIGHT: J. T. Wedgwood, after Joseph Wright of Derby, *Erasmus Darwin*, line engraving, 1820, 20.5 x 14.1.
Darwin acquired an immense literary reputation while practising as a physician. While he has become famous as the grandfather of Charles Darwin, he was an intellectual in his own right and a member of the Lunar Society, which included early industrialists such as Josiah Wedgwood. He was not a fellow of the College but a renowned medical-cum-literary man, who was based in the Midlands.

One fundamental question raised by institutional collections concerns the impulses that lie behind receiving and commissioning portraits in the first place. The desire to create a visible heritage, to encourage respect and admiration and to emulate other august bodies are certainly factors. Power, wealth and royal connections sometimes underpinned a high medical reputation and prompted the production of a likeness. So did prominence as a writer, although not necessarily on topics directly related to illness and health. Erasmus Darwin and John Moore are cases in point. Writer-physicians, such as John Armstrong, Richard Blackmore and Samuel Garth, drew upon their medical experience and became well-known literary figures. Further reasons for being depicted included the possession of fine and famous collections, a medical innovation, a discovery, research excellence, clinical acumen, organisational flair and political skills. To gather images of distinguished figures together generates and reinforces an institution's identity.

Published by Harrison & Co. May 1, 1795.

SIR RICHARD BLACKMORE.

TO do justice to injured merit, is the most pleasing duty of a biographer. That Sir Richard Blackmore had great merit, is asserted by no less men than Locke, Addison, and Dr. Johnson: yet, " by the unremit-" ted enmity of the wits, whom he provoked more by his virtue than " his dulness, his name," says the latter, " was so long used to point " every epigram on dull writers, that it became at last a bye-word of " contempt. But it deserves observation, that malignity takes hold " only of his writings, and that his life passed without reproach, even " when his boldness of reprehension naturally turned on him many " eyes desirous to espy faults, which many tongues would have made " haste to publish: but those who could not blame, could at least for-" bear to praise; and, therefore, of his private life, and domestick " character, there are no memorials." He was the son of Mr. Robert Blackmore, of Corsham, in Wiltshire. At the age of thirteen, he went to Westminster school; and, in 1668, to Oxford, where he resided thirteen years. On the 12th of April 1687, he became a Fellow of the College of Physicians, at which time he lived in Cheapside. It is singular, that his first work was an heroick poem: he was not known as a writer of verses till 1695, when he published Prince Arthur. Whatever may be the merits or defects of this poem, and it has no small quantity of both, it must have been very popular, having passed through three editions, in two years. Success attracts envy; and Dennis assailed it with a formal criticism: but it received the approbation of Locke, and the admiration of Molineux.

Our indefatigable writer, amidst all the clamour of Pope, Dryden, and the herd of inferior wits, not only published his Prince Arthur in ten books; but King Arthur, in twelve—Eliza in ten—Alfred, in twelve—the Redeemer, in six—Job, in folio—the whole book of Psalms—the Nature of Man, in three books—and his best work, Creation, a philosophical poem, in seven—with many other poems. His prose works, too, are numerous; chiefly, on religious, moral, and professional subjects.

He was knighted, by King William, in 1697, who also presented him with a gold chain and a medal, and made him one of the physicians in ordinary. These honours gave an additional stimulus to the inveteracy of the wits; who ascribed to his poetry what he owed to his politicks. In the Dedication to Alfred, he discloses, that he had a greater part in the Hanoverian succession than he had ever boasted.

He died the 8th of October 1729; and the minister who attended his death-bed testified the fervent piety of his last hours.

DR. ARMSTRONG.

ABOVE: William Holl, *John Armstrong*, 1820, stipple, 23 x 13.3. The account of Armstrong's life beneath this portrait is frank, expressing surprise about the amount of money he left and criticism of the way he lived and of a poem deemed licentious.
LEFT: Thomas Rothwell after John Vanderbank. *Richard Blackmore*, line engraving, 1795, 22.3 x 13. This print appeared in the *Biographical Magazine*. Diverse opinions of Blackmore's merits are cited and his connection with the College and King William noted. His 'fervent piety' on his deathbed receives approval. Here the close links between portraits and biographies are clear.

ABOVE: This edition of Celsus's *De Medicina* came from Matthew Baillie's library and is signed by him. Each page is 20.1 x 12. Including the binding it is 20.6 x 12.3.

LEFT: John Cochran after Henry Room, *Henry Halford*, 1838, stipple, 27.2 x 18.

Pettigrew's *Medical Portrait Gallery*, where this print appeared, included a portrait with a signature for each biography. Handwriting added authenticity to the likeness.

OPPOSITE: Artist unknown, *Francis Glisson*, c. 1670, 74 x 61.6.

Glisson became a fellow of the College in 1635 and the following year was appointed Regius Professor of Medicine at Cambridge, where he had studied at Gonville and Caius, Harvey's college. He was an active member of the College and part of the circles that led to the formation of the Royal Society of London in 1660, becoming one of its founder members. The portrait itself is most unusual in looking more like an icon than a naturalistic rendering of a person. Its provenance is unclear although it is thought to have joined the College's collection in first half of the eighteenth century. Glisson was a man of wide philosophical, medical and scientific interests.

Franciſcus · Gliſson · M · D ·

Portraits do not exist in isolation from texts, from other elements of visual and material culture, including buildings, or from public life. The connection with biography is particularly intimate; from early on in the history of printing we find them together. Examples from the *Biographical Magazine* show the physicians and poets John Armstrong and Richard Blackmore. Portraits were used as frontispieces to books, as we see in the cases of Celsus and Harvey (see page 41). Prints based on the College's portrait of Francis Glisson were used in his publications. Prints were also available to buy as freestanding items, to be placed in scrapbooks or extra-illustrated volumes or pasted onto walls. They adorned periodical and occasional publications, compilations, such as collected lives – William Pettigrew's *Medical Portrait Gallery* (1838), for example – and historical works. Over the nineteenth century portraits

The portrait of William Harvey, saved from the Great Fire of London, is precious to physicians, just as the portrait of John Hunter by Joshua Reynolds is central to the identity of the Royal College of Surgeons in London. These originals are super-charged with symbolic significance.

became yet more ubiquitous with the invention and dissemination of photography and the development of techniques for making high-quality reproductions relatively cheaply. In such ways, portraits become woven into the fabric of everyday life.

Institutions may be said to form a significant part of their identities around special portraits, generally of those who are exceptionally revered. The portrait of William Harvey, saved from the Great Fire of London, is precious to physicians, just as the portrait of John Hunter by Joshua Reynolds is central to the identity of the Royal College of Surgeons in London. These originals are super-charged with symbolic significance. However, to perform their vital cultural work, derivatives are necessary. It is precisely because iconic portraits can be copied, transformed into prints, photographed and more recently put on mugs, cards and fridge magnets, that they can insinuate themselves into the awareness of significant numbers of people, especially those who practise the same occupation.

Medical work has changed dramatically over the past five hundred years. This much is obvious since the content of medicine has altered so profoundly, and the organisational structures within which it is practised and regulated are being transformed in ways that are apparent to lay persons as well as professionals. It follows that the very label 'physician' is neither static nor clear-cut. Historians are fond of reminding their readers of the distinctions between physicians, surgeons and apothecaries, and of pointing out how many other groups have earned their living from healing. While it may be comforting to think that clear lines of demarcation existed, this is far from the truth. Individuals may change their status, just as William Hunter and Edward Jenner did in starting out as surgeons and acquiring the MD degree later on. Doctors may undertake a range of therapies, such as psychoanalysis, which is also provided by those without a medical qualification, and even 'alternative' approaches such as acupuncture. It should be clear what status any given practitioner enjoyed from, for example, their entry in the *Oxford Dictionary of National Biography*. All fellows appear in Munk's *Roll*, published from 1861 onwards and now available in a fully searchable digital form. We will also encounter physicians who were not associated with the College, yet are either present in the collections or shed light on them.

MD degrees were obtained in a variety of ways, especially in periods when there were religious restrictions on entry to an English university. Most of the medical people mentioned here appear in the *Oxford Dictionary of National Biography*, as well as Munk's *Roll*. They have been given a range of occupational designations, including by the National Portrait Gallery, an institution that has shaped British ideas of portraiture and of achievement since its foundation in 1856.

There exist a number of terms for speaking about work, each carrying distinct connotations. 'Occupation' is the most neutral, while 'vocation' and 'calling' strongly imply deep personal commitment. Although medical practice may sometimes be physically demanding, it is not usually thought of in terms of 'labour'. Rather, it is a 'profession' or a group of related professions. But 'profession' and its cognates are loaded terms, as when 'unprofessional' is used to castigate unacceptable behaviour. While sociologists debate the defining features of a profession, state regulation, exacting and meritocratic entry requirements, the possession of specialised knowledge, some notion of serving others, recognised career structures, collective identity and the punishment of mavericks are usually involved. Practitioners themselves were highly conscious of these issues, even when they used rather different concepts. Biographical accounts are rich sources on such matters and portraits too have their part to play in the cultures of professions. What constitutes 'professional' behaviour naturally depends on time and place, and it is striking to find the surgeon William Pettigrew insisting on the religious propriety of his subjects in the early Victorian period.

Portraits, then, have taken many different forms and they invite us to pay attention to the ways and places in which they are disseminated. The making of portraits needs to be contextualised too. It is partly for these reasons that provenance is so important, as is an awareness of the social processes that lie behind any given portrait. The College commissioning a portrait of its president, for example, is to be distinguished from the purchase of a work made in entirely different circumstances. In the former case we have some sense of how the process worked, who the active agents have been and what responses it has elicited. As mentioned earlier, in the past sitters and artists sometimes moved in the same circles, as was the case with John Radcliffe, Samuel Garth and Godfrey Kneller. These connections become apparent when we consider the range of sitters a given artist worked with, who purchased items in a sale after death, and who patronised any given maker. Richard Mead allowed Peter Scheemakers to use his portrait of Harvey when he commissioned a bust from him to give to the College, and gave the sculptor other jobs too. Mead was a central figure in a dining club – its membership gives us a glimpse of his associates, one of whom published a book in which a print of Harvey, based on the very same portrait, appears. When the painting came into the hands of William Hunter, it is probable that he was aware of these rich veins of patronage and friendship. Thus portraits offer a way into the textures of medical lives.

This claim remains true of later periods. John Collier, for instance, was well acquainted with the scientific and medical elites of the late nineteenth and early twentieth centuries by virtue of having married into the Huxley family; his father-in-law, Thomas Henry, had started out as a surgeon and had an interest in the visual arts, while Collier shared his dearest values. Portraits made from life arise from situations of peculiar intimacy, even when the main parties were not previously acquainted. Looking intently and being looked at repeatedly are far from easy to manage. So when a portrait is taken from life, the

Studio of Godfrey Kneller, *John Radcliffe*, c. 1710, 127 x 101.6.
Radcliffe is inextricably linked with Oxford University, and with medicine in the city, by virtue of his generous legacies. Benefactors tend to be immortalised in portraits, and the more lavish their gifts the more representations of them there tend to be. There are several versions of this painting – the College owns seven derivative prints – with three statues in Oxford itself.

personal relationships become absolutely crucial. Nigel Boonham, the sculptor responsible for the heads of Geoffrey Keynes and Cicely Saunders, is perfectly explicit on this point.[8] But it is worth remembering that portraits could still be valued even when no one had any real idea what the 'sitter' looked like, as was the case with Hippocrates, Galen, Celsus and many others. And good relationships do not necessarily produce successful portraits, while great works can arise from poor ones.

In order to set the scene, it has proved necessary to touch on many aspects of portraiture and to suggest how they lead into broad questions about the nature of occupations and institutions, the relationships between key players, the skills of artists, prevailing visual idioms, patterns of collecting, and sensitive matters around status, achievement and reputation. Portraits forge associations between people; through their presence and their uses, links are constantly refreshed. Elaborate relationships exist between the individuals depicted in the College's portraits and its life as a corporate body. It is perfectly possible to celebrate a limited number of outstanding people while affirming a collective identity. At the same time, any given portrait elicits varied and idiosyncratic reactions. These may be modified and deepened by an understanding of the contexts and personalities involved. But there is likely to remain an element of 'gut reaction', which is best avowed, insofar as this is possible. It may be prompted by knowledge of and feelings about the sitter, as well as by the portrait's visual attributes. I have sought to avoid passing judgement on the merits or likeability of the sitters. It is sometimes possible to document conflicts and vanities, alliances and affection but, when it comes to the final product, another kind of judgement, perhaps best described as 'aesthetic', is unavoidable. Questions about the quality of any given portrait are relevant, even though there can be no consensus on the matter.

Elaborate relationships exist between the individuals depicted in the College's portraits and its life as a corporate body. It is perfectly possible to celebrate a limited number of outstanding people while affirming a collective identity.

Gulielmus · HARVEY · M·D·

HARVEY

The portrait of William Harvey that hangs in the Dorchester Library occupies a special place in the life and self-image of the College. It is by an unknown hand, but is judged by Geoffrey Keynes to be an authentic likeness of a man who is arguably the most famous English physician. His discovery of the circulation of blood is likely to be the one thing most people know about him. There has been considerable debate about how and when he came to make this claim, and its originality. In so far as portraiture is concerned, however, it is necessary to focus on the ways in which images of him were valued and used, and more recently reassessed. There are three intertwined threads here. The first concerns Harvey's life and achievements, which were considerable by any standard. Second, there is his relationship with the College. The third is the role of Geoffrey Keynes, a huge admirer of Harvey, his biographer and a major player in the world of portraits.[9]

Harvey's discovery of the circulation of blood has made him a key figure in the so-called scientific revolution. Indeed he is invoked along with Galileo and Newton as an intellectual giant.[10] The actual processes by which he arrived at his ideas about circulation, like their reception, were complex. Publicly announced in *De Motu Cordis* in 1628, they had been presented and discussed in the College before then.[11] His claim elicited hostility in some circles and had no immediate effect on medical practice. The emphasis on his key achievement became strategically useful to later generations keen to demonstrate the value of scientific experiment, including on living animals, but it gives an overly narrow impression of his intellectual world. Harvey was a learned man of wide interests, including in the animal kingdom and antiquities such as Stonehenge. In addition,

OPPOSITE: Artist unknown, *William Harvey*, n.d., 133.9 x 108.5.
ABOVE: The portrait of Harvey in its usual place amid the rare books in the Dorchester Library. Picture taken in 2014. © Hélène Binet.

The bust of William Harvey by Peter Scheemakers, given to the College in 1739 by Richard Mead, is the first portrait visitors see on entering the building.

he was a royal physician and especially close to Charles I. Since Harvey had died in 1657, he was not involved in the formal inauguration of the Royal Society of London three years later, although many of its early fellows knew and revered him. His posthumous reputation was immense, and it became yet greater in contexts where the scientific method and experimental approaches were held in high esteem. Later nineteenth-century and early twentieth-century votaries of science were especially keen on him. It was precisely in these contexts that those who had made clearly delineated discoveries were turned into heroes. Portraits played a central role in such processes. At no time since his death has Harvey been neglected; there are institutions, lectures, clubs and schools named after him. A very great deal has been written about his achievements, while interest in his portraiture remains intense.

Harvey enjoyed a long and close association with the College; indeed, he was a most significant benefactor to it. However, he declined to become President. His statue was destroyed in the Great Fire – only his portrait in old age and a huge symbolic legacy survived. The post of Harveian Librarian and the annual Harveian Oration serve to keep him in the minds of generation after generation of fellows, as does the name of the College's guesthouse – William Harvey House. While he cannot be designated a 'founding father', his scientific achievements give him pride of place. The association with science is crucial, because claims to medical authority came to be grounded more in scientific research than in clinical acumen. Not that the latter is unimportant – far from it – but since Harvey's time, the commitment has steadily grown to rigorous experimental approaches for which he was a valuable figurehead.

The theme of Harvey as an experimental scientist is to be found everywhere in writings about him, and nowhere more clearly than in the work of

Geoffrey Keynes, who was trained as a surgeon. Keynes was a formidable scholar and bibliophile who wrote and collected in a wide range of areas, including the works of William Blake. He also enjoyed a long association with the National Portrait Gallery, acting as a trustee from 1942 and as chairman of the board between 1958 and 1966. Keynes was an expert on Harvey and took a special interest in his portraits; he eliminated the inauthentic ones and established the claim of a very few to show the real William Harvey.[12] The one on display in the Dorchester Library passed Keynes' stringent tests and hence it may be considered the star item in the collection. Given Keynes' ardent admiration for William Harvey and his deep knowledge of him, it is fitting that Keynes' bronze head has joined the College's collections, as well as those of the National Portrait Gallery and the Royal College of Surgeons.

The College owns other representations of Harvey, most notably the bust in the entrance hall. This was given to the College by Richard Mead, who admired Harvey a very great deal. He owned an authentic portrait of Harvey, now in the Hunterian Art Gallery in Glasgow. Hunter acquired a number of portraits depicting men of science and medicine that had been in Mead's collection, which was internationally renowned and to which he welcomed visitors. Mead was exceptionally well connected in the scholarly, artistic and literary worlds, as well as with others who shared his scientific and medical interests. Mead's portrait of Harvey was used to make two derivatives: one was the bust by Peter Scheemakers, the Flemish sculptor living in London, which graces the College's foyer. The second was a print for a publication by Thomas Birch, a close associate of Mead's and secretary of the Royal Society. Birch's *Heads of Illustrious Persons of Great Britain* was issued in parts and later as bound volumes, from 1743 to 1756. Each figure is represented by a biography and an elaborate engraving. It is significant that Harvey

Jacobus Houbraken after Godfrey Kneller, *Sir Samuel Garth*, line engraving, 1748, 35.7 x 22. This print was made for Thomas Birch's *Heads of Illustrious Persons of Great Britain* in 1748 and indicates that Jacob Tonson owned the original portrait by Kneller, which was part of the set depicting the members of the Kit-Kat Club, who were urbane men with Whig sympathies. Thus Garth should be seen in the context of prominent Whig circles. He was a practising physician, active in the College, and Harveian Orator in 1697. Also a successful poet, Garth was best known for his work *The Dispensary*, 1699, in which he discussed the fierce contemporary controversy over plans to provide free medical care to the needy, with medicines at cost price.

Attributed to Francis Hayman, *Peter Scheemakers*, c. 1739, 56 x 43.

Given the small size of the figure, this picture is best understood as a conversation piece, even though these usually contain several people. The bust and print of Harvey are recognisable. Since Richard Mead presented the bust to the College in 1739, it is assumed the painting was made around the same time. The sculptor led a long and active life; the monument to Shakespeare in Westminster Abbey, which Mead helped to organise, is by him.

was included, because most of the 'illustrious persons' were of royal, military or political importance. Many images contained not just the names of sitter, artist and engraver, but of the owner of the original portrait. As the print of Harvey mentioned Mead's collection, readers could make associations between two physicians who had never met. Thus Mead not only possessed a painting of Harvey, he was also a patron, in this case of Scheemakers, with whom he worked on a number of commissions. The picture of the sculptor, attributed to Francis Hayman and presumed to depict Scheemakers, was recently acquired by the College. It includes two derivatives – print and bust – from Mead's canvas.

Mead lived until 1754, when his collection was, at his express wish, dispersed. By that time, he had associated himself firmly with Harvey through the portrait in oils, the derivative print and the bust, and in the process he was further affirming his own links to the College, to which he also gave pieces of silver as well as acting as Censor and as Harveian Orator in 1723. Furthermore, as its second owner, he played a major role in the life of the gold-headed cane (see page 43). This served to further strengthen his connections with other physicians in the cane's life, many of whom shared his collecting interests and historical sensibilities. Askew, to whom it passed after Mead's death, is a case in point.

In 1766, the College published an edition of Harvey's works, his *Opera Omnia*, with a print, derived from the Dorchester Library portrait, as its frontispiece. The College thereby affirmed Harvey's central position in its life and self-image, while reinforcing his reputation as a learned man whose writings should be read and appreciated by those familiar with Latin. Displaying its medical and institutional past is a theme that has run through College life; portraits, whether on walls, in books, as busts or freestanding prints, are visual reminders of past and current lives.

GVILIELMI HARVEII

OPERA OMNIA:

A COLLEGIO

MEDICORVM LONDINENSI

EDITA:

MDCCLXVI.

William Harvey, *Opera Omnia*, London, 1766, 28.4 x 22.5 (platemark 24.8 x 18.2).

The College published an edition of Harvey's works, his *Opera Omnia*, with a print, derived from the Dorchester Library portrait, as its frontispiece. The College thereby affirmed Harvey's central position in its life and self-image, while reinforcing his reputation as a learned man.

DYNASTIES

One of William Macmichael's achievements in *The Gold-headed Cane*, first published anonymously in 1827, was the creation of a dynasty of prominent physicians in which one succeeded another in the fashion of monarchs, with the cane as the sceptre of office. The cane bears the coats of arms of its owners, making it a heraldic portrait of a medical lineage. Macmichael's considerable literary skills allowed him to paint vivid pictures of the lives of prominent practitioners, illustrated by portraits and other images, and by stories about them, using the voice of the cane.[13] With its profusion of anecdotes, the book brings its readers into a seemingly personal relationship with the cane's owners. Personifying the cane was a valuable device for bridging the public and domestic aspects of medical practice. Because it had privileged access to consultations and social events, it was able to paint a word picture of medical practice. The book, embellished and extended by William Munk, reminds us of the many-layered relationships that physicians enjoyed with their patients, including their most illustrious ones – members of the royal family.[14] Some prominent fellows of the College served more than one monarch, as did Harvey, Radcliffe, Mead and Halford, and this added significantly to their fame.[15]

ABOVE: Lance Calkin, *John Hughlings Jackson*, c. 1894, 83.8 x 68.6.
Jackson was one of the physicians whose reputation rested on a combination of clinical and scientific innovation. Sometimes called 'the father of English neurology', he achieved considerable international fame from modest beginnings. He is portrayed in a manner typical of his time, in dark sober attire.
OPPOSITE: Joseph Wilton, *Thomas Sydenham*, white marble, commissioned 1758, 71.1cm high.
By the 1750s, the College owned two paintings of Sydenham; that it commissioned this bust indicates the high esteem in which he was held, as the epithet 'the father of English medicine' also suggests. His status derives from the value given to meticulous clinical observation and description. Wilton enjoyed huge success as a sculptor and was a founding member of the Royal Academy.

Macmichael's considerable literary skills allowed him to paint vivid pictures of the lives of prominent practitioners, illustrated by portraits and other images, and by stories about them, using the voice of the cane.

LEFT: Francis Holl after David Martin, *William Cullen*, 1839, stipple, 19 x 11.5.
William Cullen was a celebrated Scottish physician and a renowned teacher. The classical bust, book, papers, writing accoutrements and gown all affirm his status as a learned man. This is the portrait in Pettigrew's *Medical Portrait Gallery*.
RIGHT: Henry Room, *John Baron*, c. 1838, 76.2 x 63.5.
John Baron was friendly with Matthew Baillie and Edward Jenner, publishing a laudatory biography of the latter in 1823 and 1838. This portrait was used for the derivative print in Pettigrew's *Medical Portrait Gallery*, and given to the College with portraits of the Baillie family in 1972. According to Pettigrew: 'The portraits have been selected from the most approved and authentic sources, and executed by the ablest artists. The greater number have never before appeared, and many have been expressly painted for the work by Mr. Henry Room, a very able, and most promising artist.'

Royal physicians experienced quite directly the line of succession, while creating their own lineages. In accounts of illustrious practitioners, whether biographies, memoirs or histories, portraits are repeatedly used to keep the key figures in readers' minds in ways that are similar to their use in castles, palaces and domestic settings.

One of the most powerful models for thinking about political lines comes from the family, from ideas about fatherhood and the idea of succession through male lines. We see these models adapted for use in medical and scientific circles when, for example, Hippocrates is called 'the father of medicine' and Thomas Sydenham 'the English Hippocrates'. Sydenham is elevated by association with a revered forbear, to whom he thereby stands as a worthy heir. It is a compact way of praising both men and these forms of shorthand are handy tags to which portraits form a natural complement. Such relationships were literally present in ordinary medical lives, when sons followed their fathers' occupation or were sometimes apprenticed in the early part of their training, as occurred in the career of John Hughlings Jackson.[16] Masters stood in a quasi-paternal relationship to their apprentices, while admired medical teachers – Boerhaave and Cullen spring to mind – spawned their own professional dynasties. This is not just an early modern phenomenon, as men such as Charles McMoran Wilson and John Conybeare were renowned, at least in part, for their roles in medical schools.

Neville Lewis, *John Conybeare*, c. 1950, 76.2 x 63.5.
Conybeare's portrait is one of the most distinctive in the collection. It shows Cony, as he was often called, holding a cigarette, a rare accoutrement in a portrait. A figure who elicited much affection, his reputation was derived principally from teaching and the writing of a textbook. A letter from the artist's son in the College archives explains that it was commissioned by the sitter, who is wearing the RAF tie. It was presented to the College after his death and says nothing about his medical career.

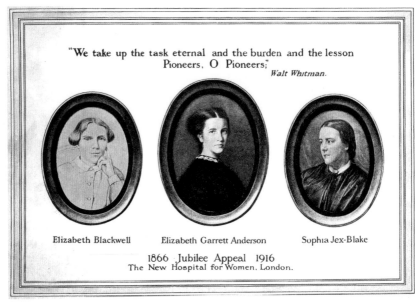

"We take up the task eternal and the burden and the lesson
Pioneers, O Pioneers,"
Walt Whitman.

Elizabeth Blackwell   Elizabeth Garrett Anderson   Sophia Jex-Blake

1866 Jubilee Appeal 1916
The New Hospital for Women, London.

Medical Women's Foundation, *The Jubilee Appeal...*, print, c. 1916, 15.5 x 23.2, Wellcome Library, London.
By placing portraits of three women doctors together, invoking their pioneer status through the words of a
prominent poet, and claiming half a century of achievement, their contributions are lauded as a basis for future
medical provision.
OPPOSITE: Attributed to Thomas Barber, *Sophia Baillie*, n.d., 75.6 x 62.9.
Sophia was the daughter of Thomas Denman, who was admitted to the College as a licentiate in midwifery in
1783. She married Matthew Baillie in 1791. In addition to giving the cane to the College, she also donated the
Zoffany picture of William Hunter lecturing at the Royal Academy. Her portrait came to the College in 1972
along with other family pictures.

Similar phenomena occurred when women became practitioners, inspired others to
follow in their footsteps and founded hospitals and teaching institutions to further the
cause of women in medicine. Ancestors beget lineages; the identities of participants
are shaped by and represented in portraits. Just as aristocratic and gentry houses
contained suites of portraits – family trees in visual form – so august organisations
display their generations of predecessors on the walls, on medals, in publications and
in their collections.

The dynastic theme emerges in other forms through the College's portrait collection,
which includes family members. This has occurred through the acquisition of works
originally intended for domestic use, which came to the College some time after
they were created. The miniatures of Robert Willan and his wife are one example;
another is the portraits of members of the Baillie family. Matthew Baillie studied at
Balliol College, Oxford, became a fellow in 1790 and built up a successful practice in
London; his patients included George III, Edward Gibbon and Walter Scott.[17] Clearly
the relationship between the Hunters and the Baillies was important in medical

Frank Bowcher, *Hermann Weber*, possibly silver, 1894, 5cm diameter.
The medal, first awarded in 1897, was created by Hermann Weber to honour the memory of Edmund
Parkes, whose *Manual of Practical Hygiene* was published in 1864. It recognises work to prevent and cure
tuberculosis, an area of interest for Weber. Weber himself is on one side, a classical scene designed by him
on the other. Parkes, who was much loved, had died in 1876.

Just as aristocratic and gentry houses contained suites of portraits – family trees in visual form – so august organisations display their generations of predecessors on the walls, on medals, in publications and in their collections.

circles, partly because William and John Hunter, Matthew's uncles, were renowned collectors, teachers and anatomists. Matthew's relationship with William was especially close. The father of Sophia, Matthew's wife, was also a medical man, and her twin sister married the ill-fated accoucheur Sir Richard Croft, who committed suicide in 1818. It was Sophia who presented the cane and Zoffany's picture of William Hunter at the Royal Academy to the College. Matthew's sister was the well-known poet Joanna Baillie. Such relationships were common knowledge, because newspapers, magazines, memoirs and so on refer to them, thereby satisfying a strong curiosity about those in the public eye. A woman who published successfully was certainly the object of interest. Here we touch on the theme of celebrity, which is now distinguished from the fame that comes from high-level skills, achievements and socially valuable contributions. 'Celebrity' implies a public persona, regardless of whether

ABOVE: Johann Zoffany, *William Hunter at the Royal Academy,* c. 1772 , 77.4 x 103.5, frame 125 x 98. William Hunter became Professor of Anatomy at the Royal Academy in 1769, a position that bridged the medical and artistic worlds. Zoffany was born in Frankfurt and arrived in England in 1760. An artist of range and originality, Zoffany occupied a central place in London's cultural life, working for the royal family, as did Hunter. This picture was given to the College in 1825 by Sophia Baillie – her late husband Matthew was William Hunter's heir.

or not the possessor discharges an occupation to an exceptionally high standard.[18] Some celebrity works by association, of which there was certainly an element when practitioners attended prominent members of society. As medical men achieved fame beyond their specialised world, their position was frequently recognised by portraits and publications, and discussion of their close relationships occurred, whether these were familial or only metaphorically so. Derivative prints disseminated likenesses of celebrities and the famous, as photographs have since the middle of the nineteenth century.

My comments on the cane indicated that dynasty may be a useful metaphor for the ways in which medical success is transmitted through generations, enabling it to be recognised by others. This is not incompatible with meritocratic values, especially if training occurs within families or small, close-knit communities. This could be a family business, for example running a general practice or an institution, as happened with the Monros at Bethlem Hospital and at their private madhouse, Brooke House, Clapton. Medical schools, particularly when strong-minded figures such as Moran were involved,

Photographer unknown, *William Osler in Edward Jenner's chair in the room of the Regius Professor of Medicine, University Museums, Oxford,* n.d., Wellcome Library, London.
By being photographed in Jenner's chair, Osler enacts his admiration of a figure who appears in his 'Bibliotheca Prima', the list of those medical writings he considered most significant and groundbreaking. He is the quintessential learned man.

contained intense relationships between those who provided training and their disciples – this word, with its religious connotations, is fully justified by the admiration, sometimes hero-worship, that a few physicians have inspired, and by the desire to collect items associated with them, which are sometimes treated as relics. Indeed portraits themselves can be seen as relics.[19]

Values are handed down between generations, along with items that enable people to remember those they most admire. These may be portraits, which are acting as 'souvenirs' alongside other objects, such as specimens of handwriting, personal accoutrements, chairs, even overcoats.[20] Accordingly, the ability to collect and document artefacts and images underpins the ways in which portraits and ancillary objects work. As objects of memory are used, emotional meanings are collected too. The great bibliophile William Osler had a strong sense of his debt to his own teachers, and his students and colleagues felt the same. Three admirers assembled a *Checklist of Osleriana* in 1976, opening the book with some lines that Osler had used to refer to his teacher R. Palmer Howard:

> *Whatever way my days decline*
> *I felt and feel, though left alone*
> *His being working in mine own.*
> *The footsteps of his life in mine.[21]*

Portraits prompt and fashion such vivid sentiments, which underpin dynasties.

ABOVE: Joyce Aris, after Stephen Seymour Thomas, *William Osler*, 1960, 116.8 x 91.4.

There are many portraits in a range of media of Osler and this one, painted in Paris by the American artist Seymour Thomas in 1908, shows the sitter in a thoroughly familiar format – seated, book in hand, with other accoutrements of study clearly visible. Joyce Aris copied a number of paintings for the College, showing yet again that when originals were not available, copies could still convey the sitters' prestige. In 1908 Osler had been Regius Professor of Medicine at Oxford for nearly four years.

LEFT: Photographer unknown, *Stephen Seymour Thomas standing next to his portrait of Sir William Osler*, n.d., Wellcome Library, London.

The actual painting of the portrait took Seymour Thomas only eleven hours. Osler liked the result. The artist kept it until 1955, shortly before his death.

INHERITANCE, SALES, GIFTING AND COLLECTING

The notion of inheritance is a powerful one, whether it is applied literally to the passing down of goods through generations or figuratively to the transmission of ideas, practices and forms of culture. Both senses of the term are relevant to the College's portrait collections. Practices of giving gifts are inseparable from these themes; they become heirlooms to be passed on when the recipient dies. Books often contain clear evidence to support these points, because owners write their names in and annotate them, while they may well contain portraits that provide visual prompts of affinities between people. As we saw, Matthew Baillie wrote his name on the title page of a book by Celsus, which faces the portrait frontispiece (see page 30).

When Richard Mead died, his books, prints, medals, coins and paintings were sold, in contrast to Hans Sloane, whose collections formed the basis for the British Museum. Those who bought items in the sale could still feel a pride in the connection, even if a financial transaction had been involved. Similarly, in giving items made from silver to the College, Mead ensured that those who used them after his death could feel his continued presence in the institution's life. There are many ways in which any given medical generation receives achievements and artefacts from earlier ones, and transmits what is precious to them to future ones.

Once again, the gold-headed cane neatly illustrates these themes. Mead had inherited it, along with his practice and house, from John

OPPOSITE: Thomas Murray, *Hans Sloane*, c. 1725, 125.1 x 99.1.
Sloane became President of the College in 1719 and held the post for sixteen years. In 1727 he also became President of the Royal Society, following the death of Sir Isaac Newton, serving for fourteen years. He remains the only person to have held both positions simultaneously. His wide interests and extraordinary collections demonstrate the central roles physicians could play in the capital's cultural life.

Radcliffe, and he passed it on to Anthony Askew who was, like Mead, a noted collector and scholar. The relationships between physicians existed at many levels, from shared friendships and institutional affiliations to scholarly passions and commercial transactions. It is significant that these relationships occurred within medical circles, where they bridged sharp religious, political and social divides. When John Freind spent some time in prison, Mead gave him a copy of Daniel Le Clerc's *History of Physic*, first published in French in 1696; Freind's own book on the subject was dedicated to Mead – yet their religious and political values were miles apart. The rhetorical potential of claims that medical men could work harmoniously together, no matter what their beliefs and commitments were, should not be underestimated.

The rhetorical potential of claims that medical men could work harmoniously together, no matter what their beliefs and commitments were, should not be underestimated.

Askew was a famous book collector, especially of editions of classical works. He also acquired prints, drawing and manuscripts. The printed catalogues that listed his possessions before their sale are instructive. Askew owned many portraits in the form of prints, as well as numerous works with portrait frontispieces, such as Harvey's *Opera Omnia*. His reading and collecting were eclectic, and included travel works, reference books, pamphlets, historical tomes, sermons and medical works, from Hippocrates and Celsus to writings by his contemporaries. Thus portraits abounded in his collections; as a result, seeing faces, reading their owners' words and in many cases having close and direct personal associations with them, including in the College, were intricately entwined.[22]

ABOVE: Unknown artist, *John Freind*, boxwood, n.d., 17.8 x 12.7.
Freind is shown as a classical figure, with toga, clasp and short hair. There is a monument to Freind in Westminster Abbey with a similarly classicising bust; the inscription mentions his command of Latin.
OPPOSITE: After Michael Dahl, *John Freind*, c. 1725, 124.5 x 99.1.
There are several versions of Freind's portrait and the provenance of this one is unclear before it was given to the College in 1879. The bust of Hippocrates, together with paper and inkstand suggested a learned physician. Freind's *History of Physic*, published 1725–6, amply revealed his historical knowledge. A successful medical practitioner and classical scholar who published extensively, Freind was a controversial figure, including in his religious and political affiliations, given his Jacobite associations.

It is worth emphasising the depth of scholarship manifested by many of the physicians associated with the College and the profound feelings inspired in them by those they studied.

ABOVE: Allan Ramsay, *Anthony Askew*, 1750, 124.5 x 101.6, Emmanuel College, Cambridge.
OPPOSITE: Artist unknown, *John Fothergill*, n.d., 54.6 x 43.2. This portrait is reminiscent of the conversation pieces that were popular in the eighteenth century. The figure takes up a relatively small amount of space and the overall effect is one of austerity. Fothergill was a Quaker, with scientific interests and fine collections, which included plants, shells and minerals, funded by his successful medical practice. The collections attracted considerable attention, including from foreign visitors. The College owns six prints of Fothergill, none of them derived from this painting. This number suggests the interest he attracted both during and after his lifetime.

The combination of learning and medicine, then, is neatly exemplified by Askew, who was portrayed by Allan Ramsay, the Scottish painter in the circle of Richard Mead. Other physicians had similar interests to Askew's, even if few possessed his resources. The eighteenth century saw several such men rise to prominence: Sloane, Mead and Fothergill, for instance. It is hard to exaggerate the importance of either the value of learning for the status and self-understanding of physicians, at least until the twentieth century, or the affinities between collecting and medical practice that have endured and shaped the culture of the College. It is worth emphasising the depth of scholarship manifested by many of the physicians associated with the College and the profound feelings inspired in them by those they studied. These arose from a blend of desiring to emulate high achievement with recognising their very real debt to the most outstanding earlier figures; these sentiments were at once intellectual and emotional. Yet it was perfectly possible to be as serious as Askew, without becoming an intellectual hero to later generations, as Harvey, Sydenham, Edward Jenner and Thomas Young were for Osler.[23] Each generation made judgements about their forbears; those admired for their scholarship were not necessarily medically significant, just as those who did sterling service for the College were not necessarily distinguished as scientists or even clinicians. And because the criteria underpinning these judgements were never stable, a complex picture results. Probing not just portraits, but the webs of affinity in which they are enmeshed, helps us to understand better the history of medicine and of the College.

There are two notable portraits of Anthony Askew. The first is present in the College only in the form of a derivative print, made by Thomas Hodgetts in 1811. The original hangs in Emmanuel College, Cambridge, where Askew was a student. It was painted in 1750, the year in which Askew took his MD, by Allan Ramsay, who had depicted Richard Mead three years earlier (see page 19).[24] The latter work was not destined for a private collection, but was hung in the Foundling Hospital where it could be seen by members of the public. Mead was famously generous in allowing visitors to view his collection and was noted for his hospitality, as was Askew. Who owned what was hardly a secret. Sale catalogues after the owner's death made this fully public, and while they were alive, word of mouth and correspondence were effective means of communication. In any case, some derivative prints indicated who owned the original, as was the case in the *Heads of Illustrious Persons*. Hence Mead's fame as a collector lived on in the memories of those who knew him and owned artefacts that were once his, in sales catalogues and in such prints. For example, we know that Osler owned the published lists of both Askew's and Mead's book collections, as well as works by the latter. Ramsay like Mead had royal connections. Askew is shown as a graceful young man, in a manner fully in keeping with Ramsay's depictions of other elite men in the mid-eighteenth century. The open book is an edition in Greek of Hippocrates' *On Humours*.

In contrast, the College's likeness is a small and extremely fragile piece of unbaked clay made by a Chinese modeller; it shows a stout man seated and holding the cane. Whereas Ramsay's work is elegant and refined, an oil of substantial size, Chitqua's is a small, squat statuette. It has considerable curiosity value, not least because works by Chitqua, who was in England between 1769 and 1772, are extremely rare. It illustrates a fundamental point about portraiture – a single individual can be represented in diverse ways and still be recognisable. The portrait was given

> It illustrates a fundamental point about portraiture – a single individual can be represented in diverse ways and still be recognisable.

OPPOSITE: Chitqua, *Anthony Askew*, polychrome unbaked clay, c. 1770, 33cm high.

Baillie was comfortable with portraits for the use of family and friends but not, it seems, when they were circulated more publicly. This reveals something of the power of print, the intense anxiety about the reputation of physicians and the ways in which this was meticulously fashioned.

ABOVE: Henry Bone, after John Hoppner, *Matthew Baillie*, enamel, 1810, 12 x 9.5.
An old ink label on the backing board states that the enamel cost forty-five guineas, and the frame seven. The College also owns a painting of Baillie by Hoppner, but the precise date is unknown. There was a derivative print in existence by 1809.

to the College by Askew's daughter Lady Pepys in 1831, becoming one of its most remarkable possessions. Presumably she inherited it from her father.

The Baillie family illustrates many of the themes of this book. We have already noted three key points: Matthew Baillie's links with his uncles, William and John Hunter; his widow's gift of Zoffany's work and the cane; and the connections with other medical families through marriage. In the early 1970s, a descendant presented a number of family pictures to the College, showing that even later generations valued their connections with it; the College in turn saw the importance of owning pictures of spouses, siblings and children. Thus its relationship has been not just with the physician, but also with their close relatives. Matthew Baillie died in 1823 at the age of sixty-two, exhausted, apparently, by his demanding professional life. Two years later the surgeon James Wardrop published a two-volume edition of his works, embellished with portraits. His detailed life of Baillie is instructive, and not just about Baillie himself, as it skilfully presents general precepts about medical practice and professional conduct, of which its subject was an admirable exemplar. Thus biography is shown to be a valuable exercise, while members of the medical profession display 'moral character' especially well: 'the honour and integrity of the physician ... is deservedly entitled to public gratitude and respect'. As portraits and biography go hand in hand, it is not surprising to find Wardrop describing Baillie's physical appearance. But it is striking to learn that Baillie 'shrunk from having any likeness of himself, during his lifetime, intruded on the public'. Wardrop then recounts Baillie's dismay at finding out that a print had been made of his portrait by Hoppner. He purchased the plate and issued legal threats should copies be made and circulated. Baillie is described as having 'a particular dislike to the idea of seeing his face in the window of a print shop!'[25] There are several portraits of him and six prints in the possession of the College, some produced after his death. Baillie was comfortable with portraits for the use of family and friends but not, it seems, when they were circulated more publicly. This reveals something of the power of print, the intense anxiety about the reputation of physicians and the ways in which this was meticulously fashioned.

Collecting has been integral to many medical lives. Possessions gave pleasure and solace, they aided scientific and clinical work, they provided a focus for sociability, and in some cases they formed the kernel of great museums that remain outstanding today. When they were not kept, for whatever reason, details of them became known through published catalogues and sometimes display. In any case, well-known collectors were objects of interest in their own right, and the most hospitable ones disseminated ideas as they welcomed visitors and shared their tables. This account applies to Osler, who died in 1919, just as it does to Mead, Askew, Sloane, Fothergill, William and John Hunter in the eighteenth century.

SCIENCE AND THE BEDSIDE

William Harvey has proved to be of enduring importance to later generations largely thanks to his scientific achievements – that is, his use of methods and approaches that resonated with later generations of medical men keen on experiment and the scientific method. It is well known that the term 'science' has a complex history, carrying a wide range of shifting connotations. Is medicine wholly part of science, or do its clinical subtleties mean that it is deeply akin to the humanities and social sciences? There can be no definitive answers to such a question, but the changing roles of laboratory-based work and of social approaches in modern medicine remain important areas of historical inquiry. Charles Dodds, President of the College in the 1960s, was the first man to hold the post who was not a clinician, yet the relationships between science and medicine were a subject of keen interest long before then. The presidents have in fact displayed quite diverse forms of professional distinction. For example, a more recent president, and the first woman to hold the post, Margaret Turner-Warwick, describes in *Living Medicine* how she brought a strong commitment to patient care to the post.

In the past it was common for distinguished exponents of natural philosophy to have received a medical education. The prominent Scot James

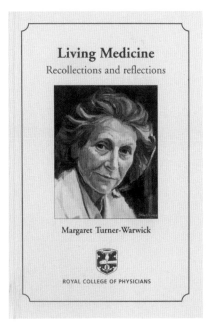

ABOVE: The cover of Margaret Turner-Warwick's memoir, *Living Medicine*, published by the College in 2005, uses a portrait of her by Jeff Stultiens, who also painted Carol Black, the second female President. Turner-Warwick describes the election process and her approach to the organisation of the College.

OPPOSITE: Raymond Piper, *Charles Dodds*, 1967, 96.2 x 71.1.

This sideways pose is unusual and, although it is impossible to see Dodds' full face, the portrait is evocative, suggesting a busy, purposeful person. He holds a sheet on which a molecular structure is clearly visible – a synthetic oestrogen that he discovered. Whether in two or three dimensions, representations of molecules in portraits are widely recognised as signs of scientific achievement.

Printed by Sir Thos Lawrence P.R.A.   Engraved by G. Adcock

THOMAS YOUNG, M.D., F.R.S., F.L.S. &c. &c.

ABOVE: George Adcock after Thomas Lawrence, *Thomas Young*, stipple, 1830, 22.8 x 14.5.
This plate, complete with the authenticating signature that shows he is an officer of the Royal Society,
appeared in William Jerdan's *National Portrait Gallery of Illustrious and Eminent Personages of the Nineteenth
Century: with memoirs*. This work in five volumes (1830–34) reveals that the idea of a national portrait gallery
was present in books before the London institution was founded in 1856. Lawrence had painted Young some
time after 1820.

A common approach was to present the physician seated with books, and it endured for a long time.

Hutton, sometimes seen as the 'father of geology', who had trained as a physician, is a case in point. Another example is Thomas Young, who was as much a 'scientist' as he was a physician.[26] Young was a veritable polymath, a distinguished fellow of the College and of the Royal Society. Pettigrew's *Medical Portrait Gallery* (1838), in which Young features, as do many other figures mentioned in this volume, discussed the relationships between medicine, broadly defined to include the author's own field, surgery and science. Its title stressed that the biographical memoirs concerned not only 'the most celebrated' but also those who had 'contributed to the advancement of medical science'. Pettigrew does not explain what he means by 'medical science', and his accounts are shot through with comments about moral character, professional duties and the social value of medical men. Viewed in this light, his selection may appear odd since, in addition to the usual suspects – Hippocrates, Harvey and Halford, for instance – many of the figures he selected are scarcely known or studied today.

Medical practice was one way of earning a living and of receiving institutional recognition when there were few such opportunities for those with scientific interests. For medics there were opportunities for training and apprenticeships, institutions with honorary positions, especially in the wake of the voluntary hospital movement, which took hold over the eighteenth century, and plenty

of patients willing to pay for their healthcare.[27] A few physicians became very rich indeed, as can be discerned from their 'wealth at death' given in the *Oxford Dictionary of National Biography*. Such work could help to subsidise more scientific activities, and in any case, there can be no firm dividing lines between, say, chemistry, the life sciences, pharmacy and medicine, even as the names and remits of such fields change. Yet taking all these points into account, Young's interests and achievements were still exceptionally broad, embracing optics, hieroglyphics, nosology, vision and colour theory; he was an accomplished musician who also undertook administrative roles in scientific and medical establishments. Commentators seem to agree that he was not an especially successful clinician. Conversations about the relationships between clinical success, research achievements, teaching distinction and organisational-cum-political flair are not likely to cease any time soon. Their intricacy suggests some of the challenges that portrait artists faced when choosing how to depict physicians.

A common approach was to present the physician seated with books, and it endured for a long time, surfacing, for instance in John Collier's portrait of William Munk (1898; see page 22). It was well established by the seventeenth century. Munk was no scientist, but Michael Foster, his younger contemporary, also painted by Collier, certainly was. Munk was a

The study and the classroom provided suitable settings for portraits of scientific and medical innovators, who were thereby visually associated with scholarly traditions rather than with the laboratory.

successful physician and writer, especially in the field of biography – his *Life of Sir Henry Halford* (1895) should be considered alongside his *Roll of the Royal College of Physicians*, first published in 1861. By contrast, Foster, painted only a few years later in 1907, just before his death, is presented quite differently; he is expounding – standing up, chalk in hand – on a subject that is clearly 'scientific', judging by the marks on the blackboard. It is precisely because the artist had married into the family of Thomas Henry Huxley – a prominent figure promoting the value of science, who was close to Michael Foster – that we can be confident that Collier was well aware of the visual idioms that were appropriate for the depiction of men in the scientific and medical worlds in the late nineteenth and early twentieth centuries.[28] It is striking then that he generally opted for a visually conservative approach, showing men in sober dress and with few accoutrements, or even none at all. This is not altogether surprising given the ferocity of debates about, for example, vivisection, a practice that was sometimes justified by invoking William Harvey's work, which could be presented as *experimental* physiology or medicine.[29] Thus the study and the classroom provided suitable settings for portraits of scientific and medical innovators, who were thereby visually associated with scholarly traditions rather than with the laboratory.

Just as 'science' posed challenges to portrait artists depicting its most distinguished exponents, so did clinical activities, since it was rarely possible to show the sitters carrying out their work. This aspect of medical practice has been captured by photography, while painted portraits remain largely wedded to the depiction of a single seated figure. It was possible for biographies to stress the scientific dimensions of medical practice, and for participation in the Royal Society to become a clearer signifier of scientific credentials as it became more the

OPPOSITE: John Collier, *Michael Foster*, 1907, 144 x 105, National Portrait Gallery, London. The portrait was given to the Gallery in 1920 by the sitter's son, also Michael, who was a fellow of the College. Michael *père* was the son of a doctor, awarded the MD degree in 1859, and had served as a ship's surgeon.

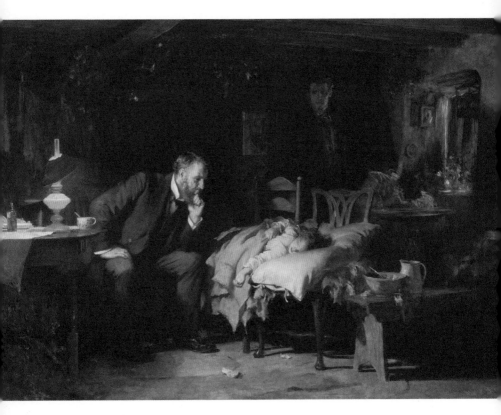

ABOVE: Luke Fildes, *The Doctor,* exhibited 1891, Tate, frame 207.5 x 287.5.

The Doctor ... has become one of the most widely known and best-loved images of medical practice.

domain of professionals than of gentlemen amateurs over the nineteenth century.[30] As the example of William Osler makes clear, there was no inherent tension between a profound commitment to scientific research and a high level of clinical sophistication on the one hand, and deep humanistic scholarship on the other. Painted portraits of Osler did not seek to capture the bedside manner for which he was so renowned.

One artist, however, did attempt to express something about clinical attentiveness, even if his picture was not a portrait in the narrowest sense of that term. Because much is known about his career and experiences, and because he also painted one of the royal portraits in the College's collection, Luke Fildes' life and work can be used to illustrate a number of important themes.

After Luke Fildes, *The Doctor*, 1895, photogravure, 55 x 76, in frame 86.5 x 112.8.
The popularity of Fildes' painting encouraged the production of derivatives. This one was made in France by Goupil
& Cie, a leading firm of art dealers, who made fine reproductions of paintings and sculpture. It was given to the
College by a fellow; this illustration shows the copy in the Wellcome Library. Credit: Wellcome Library, London.

In 1890, Henry Tate commissioned Fildes to paint a picture on a subject of
his choosing. The artist was already known for his compassionate images of
contemporary social conditions. He chose to depict a medical scene, and *The Doctor*
was exhibited the following year. It has become one of the most widely known and
best-loved images of medical practice. The College owns a fine print of this painting
made in France in 1895, and Fildes' portrait of Edward VII was acquired in 1906.

This influential artist can shed light on royal patronage, medical practitioners and
their most powerful clients. Fildes' portrait of Edward VII was painted in 1905, and
although considerably smaller, it is virtually identical to the state portrait of 1902. The
sitter had been made an honorary fellow of the College in 1897. Close connections
with the reigning monarch and their court have characterised the College since its

inception. Treating members of a royal family is far from straightforward, since there is a chance that the doctor will be blamed for any bad outcome, as happened, for instance, to John Radcliffe. Thus the prestige of serving such elevated patients is offset by the public vulnerability that is inevitably incurred in the process. Artists in receipt of royal patronage may find themselves in similarly complex situations. The same painters sometimes depicted members of the medical professions. Each artist's set of relationships, like each physician's, was distinctive.

Fildes' canvas *The Doctor* portrays a man who stands for caring practitioners of the period. Given its immense popularity, the work illustrates something significant about medics' senses of themselves, about the ways they could be envisioned at a specific moment in time, and about the artist's engagement with medicine. Fildes and his wife lost their young son, Philip, in 1877 and were struck by the way his illness was handled by a Dr Murray. According to one of their surviving sons: 'the character and bearing of their doctor throughout the time of their anxiety made a deep impression on my parents. Dr Murray became the symbol of professional devotion...'[31]

While some have seen *The Doctor* as sentimental, it captured not just a common situation – childhood mortality remained high in this period – but the role a practitioner could play, and be seen to play, in serious illness. Perhaps the picture is better described as idealistic, in that it constructs a central role for the doctor in a modest domestic setting, a role in which he manifests concern and compassion. Naturally, in practice the roles of medical men varied considerably, so the painting, by an artist concerned about prevailing social conditions, evokes a desirable scenario.

L. V. Fildes published a biography of his father in 1968 – some forty years after his death. The book, which draws extensively on letters and diaries, was designed to show his father in a

Close connections with the reigning monarch and their court have characterised the College since its inception. Treating members of a royal family is far from straightforward, since there is a chance that the doctor will be blamed for any bad outcome.

OPPOSITE: Luke Fildes, *Edward VII*, 1905, 84.5 x 66.7

Certain themes are ubiquitous with respect to portraiture practices – the importance of sittings, the quality of the relationship between artists and sitters, and sensitivities about appearance.

positive light and is valuable precisely because it foregrounds the artist's experiences of his work, reactions to it, and the politics of the art world at the time. It not only recounts the process of painting *The Doctor*, but also provides a detailed account of Fildes' relations with the royal family, several members of whom he painted. Certain themes are ubiquitous with respect to portraiture practices – the importance of sittings, the quality of the relationship between artists and sitters, and sensitivities about appearance, for instance. These are likely to be articulated more fully in the case of prominent sitters and artists.

There is a sequel to this story. When Edward VII died aged sixty-nine after a short illness, Fildes was summoned to the Palace to draw him on his deathbed. His privileged access to the dead King's body is striking. Fildes' sketch was published in *The Graphic*, a publication with which he had been closely associated for many years. He subsequently made a replica of his formal portrait of the King for Queen Alexandra's private use. One recurrent motif here is the forms of intimacy both artists and medical practitioners enjoy, which constitutes a particular type of privilege, while making them vulnerable at the same time. More generally, it is worth noting the power of the highest form of patronage for organisations – the *Royal* Academy of Arts and the *Royal* College of Physicians, for example – whose value is constantly being negotiated. Luke Fildes' life and work help us to appreciate the social contexts in which art and medicine were practised, which, through the complicated relationships they involve, provide their exponents with experiences that shape their careers.

The point here is not just that the medical and artistic worlds overlapped, especially in London and among elite practitioners, but that their lived experiences made a significant contribution to their work both as individuals and in corporate bodies.

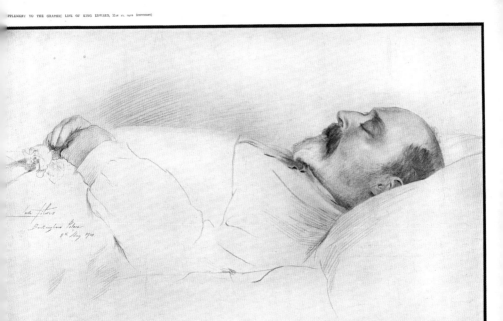

ABOVE: Luke Fildes, *King Edward VII*, 1910, relief halftone, 42 x 62.5, National Portrait Gallery, London. *The Graphic* published Fildes' work in May 1910, only a few days after the King's death.

GENDER

The Doctor shows a soberly clad man who could be seen as a benign paternal figure; an older, experienced person keeping watch over a younger vulnerable one. John Collier's portraits from the same time also show men in dark clothes, in suitably sedate surroundings. There is clearly a form of masculinity being portrayed in such cases and it is worth asking about comparable types of femininity, since the second half of the nineteenth century saw the advent of women in professional medicine – a development that caused fierce controversy. Female physicians were admitted to the College relatively late, and this is reflected in the small number of portraits in the collection that depict them.

Portrait artists are used to finding the right pictorial devices for any particular commission. 'Right' here means not 'correct', but 'apt' or 'suitable for the occasion'. The arrival of women as medical practitioners in the mid-nineteenth century presented a new challenge for artists. In the case of Elizabeth Garrett Anderson, the first woman to qualify in England, John Singer Sargent showed a sober figure in an academic gown – the gown was at her request. There is a story that he begged her to wear a piece of jewellery and so she put on a cheap pearl necklace costing sixpence. Then there was the issue of her hands. Sargent more or less hid one of them, but the other is more elegant and tapered than Anderson's own. The canvas is quite unlike his portraits of society women, so often garbed in evening dress and looking like birds of paradise. As his *oeuvre* makes clear, Sargent depicted a number of professional men, including doctors such as William Osler. They too are depicted soberly and sometimes gowned like Anderson.[32] She was sixty-four at the time the portrait was painted and is shown seated, in an

Female physicians were admitted to the College relatively late, and this is reflected in the small number of portraits in the collection that depict them.

OPPOSITE: John Singer Sargent, *Elizabeth Garrett Anderson*, 1900, 83.8 x 66. Courtesy of Mrs Jennifer Loehnis; on loan to the National Portrait Gallery, London.

As more women became prominent in public life, the appropriate way to depict successful professional women had to be considered by portrait artists, more of whom were also women.

interior, with a look of calm confidence. This work remained in the family and has only recently gone on public display. Sargent, a painter of exceptional inventiveness, insight and virtuosity, in effect portrayed Anderson as if she were a man. As more women became prominent in public life, the appropriate way to depict successful professional women had to be considered by portrait artists, more of whom were also women. The two portraits in the collection by women artists – Mary Beale and Mary Black from the seventeenth and eighteenth centuries respectively – are rare examples of such work. It is only in the twentieth century that women have become prominent as portrait painters.

Victoria Crowe's portrait of Janet Vaughan was purchased by the National Portrait Gallery in 1987, shortly after it was completed. Vaughan, who was related to Henry Halford, studied physiology at Oxford, did her clinical training in London, and became a clinical pathologist. Her career included research and also academic administration. She was Principal of Somerville College, Oxford, for twenty-two years – the first married woman, one furthermore with children, to hold the post. Above all a scientist, she became a fellow of the College in 1939, and in 1943 the first woman to be admitted to the Council.[33] Depicted towards the end of her life, she is shown in a domestic setting that is reminiscent of Maggie Hambling's portrait of Dorothy Hodgkin, painted in 1985. Hodgkin, a few years younger than Vaughan, and still the only British woman to have won a Nobel Prize for science, also enjoyed a long association with Somerville. Portraits of accomplished women in

OPPOSITE: Victoria Crowe, *Janet Vaughan*, 1986–7, 81.3 x 66, National Portrait Gallery, London © Victoria Crowe, reproduced with permission.

After Mary Beale, *Thomas Sydenham*, n.d., 76.2 x 63.5.
This picture closely resembles the painting in the National Portrait Gallery, where the artist is given as Mary Beale, England's first professional woman portrait painter, and dated 1688. Sydenham was a Parliamentarian in the civil war.

Mary and Thomas Black, *Messenger Monsey*, 1764, 127 x 101.6.
This is one of the most striking portraits in the College's collections, with its light tones and informal
air. Nonetheless it contains many of the elements expected in portraits of physicians, who were often
represented, as here, seated with a book and in a reflective pose. This is Mary Black's only known portrait and
Monsey refused to pay for it. It reached the College in 1877, presented by a donor whose family had inherited
it from Mary Black. Monsey was something of an eccentric, who left his body for dissection at a time when
fear of grave-robbing for just such a purpose was rife.

TOP: David Poole, *Margaret Turner-Warwick*, 1992, 89.5 x 69.
ABOVE: Paul Brason, *Ian Gilmore*, 2013, 112 x 93 including frame.
Gilmore was President between 2006 and 2010, and chose an informal mode for the portrait that is now customary at the end of the term of office. Brason has painted many senior academics and those in public life.
OPPOSITE: Fred Wicker, *Dorothy Hare*, c. 1955, 97.2 x 71.7.

a domestic environment affirm their female status, which is played down in Sargent's painting of Anderson. College-commissioned portraits are necessarily somewhat different, since their main intention is to represent the sitter as office-holder.

David Poole's portrait of Margaret Turner-Warwick makes this perfectly explicit, through her robes and the caduceus across her lap. The custom of showing distinguished professionals seated and inside becomes a trifle more informal when presidents are painted without a gown or signs of office, as Carol Black, and a number of recent male presidents, have chosen to be. Men's and women's clothing remains distinct, so that darkish jackets and ties with a shirt become a kind of male uniform, next to which female attire stands out because it tends to be more vibrant in colour, and diverse in texture, and may be complemented by jewellery. In this context the portrait of Dorothy Hare, herself an amateur painter, is notable. She too is seated and begowned, but the artist has incorporated three distinctive elements. Her gown is presented not just in vibrant colours, but as a major element of the composition. Hare sits not in a chair with arms, but on a stool, and seen from the side, which allows the gown to form a prominent part of the portrait. The stool and wall chime with the red of the gown. Then there is the building – the University of London's Senate House – clearly recognisable in the background. With these elements combined, an unusual and striking picture has resulted, without it being in any way conventionally 'feminine'. Hare became a fellow of the College

The commissioning process can be a delicate one, since artist and sitter need to spend time together and develop a productive relationship, if possible. Carol Black, the second female president, was the prime mover in the choice of Jeff Stultiens to paint her.

ABOVE: Julia Fullerton-Batten, *Carol Black,* 2006, C-type colour print, National Portrait Gallery, London. Black is shown in the Censors' Room surrounded by portraits, one hand resting on Annigoni's picture of Lord Moran. The photograph formed part of an exhibition at the Portrait Gallery, *A Picture of Health.* OPPOSITE: Jeff Stultiens, *Carol Black,* 2006, 127 x 102. The sitter was President 2002–6.

in 1936, only the third woman to do so. Her career demonstrates a strong interest in the welfare of women. Painted around 1955, this portrait suggests an inventive hand, although the artist in question, Frederick John Hayes Wicker, is not well known. It should be stressed that the portrait of Hare was not commissioned by the College, but presented as a gift in 1968, a year after her death, by her niece and nephew.

The commissioning process can be a delicate one, since artist and sitter need to spend time together and develop a productive relationship, if possible. Carol Black, the second female president, was the prime mover in the choice of Jeff Stultiens to paint her – he had already painted Margaret Turner-Warwick, although not for the College. Black knew that she didn't want to be painted in a gown or with a symbol of office, and was unable to come up with a suitable background.[34] In the end, she is shown seated in a pale armchair against a background that is cloud-like, wearing a large necklace. Although her trousers and top are black, the picture is predominantly light in tone and it portrays her in a recognisably feminine manner. While she is presented as confidently in command of the situation, there are no references to

Catherine Goodman, *Cicely Saunders*, 2005, 91.2 x 70.7, National Portrait Gallery, London.

With more women rising to prominence as portrait painters, fresh ways of imagining female achievement will emerge.

her occupation and so an uninformed viewer might interpret the painting as depicting a woman with self-possession, but glean little more from it. This is indeed an aspect of portraits devoid of accoutrements, where the setting in which they are displayed has to do a great deal of work. There are few depictions of women in the College's collections; the more recent ones show those who are particularly prominent in the institution. With more female presidents, the possible comparisons will be greater, revealing as much about how artists see powerful professional women as about those women themselves.

A useful case study in this context is provided by Cicely Saunders, who became a fellow in 1974. Saunders provided the driving energy for the hospice movement, achieving worldwide fame in the process. She was a forceful practitioner who had already trained as an almoner and nurse before undertaking medical studies, an inspirational writer and speaker, a determined organiser and an exemplar of compassion.[35] The National Portrait Gallery commissioned a young artist, Catherine Goodman, to paint Saunders as she was dying. The picture was unveiled – in her presence – shortly before her death. Painter and subject forged a close relationship and Saunders' comment to the effect that the portrait was as much her work as the artist's is often quoted. There is a profound truth in her observation, which insists on a process of active collaboration between the two main parties involved. The end result does not evoke a person whose life is ebbing away, but a woman of insight and focus. Her femininity, if that is the right term, is signalled through her hair, necklace and clothing, but it is in no way stereotypical. Whether we can attribute this to the artist also being female is difficult to say, but it is distinctly possible that with more women rising to prominence as portrait painters, fresh ways of imagining female achievement will emerge.

The College's 2001 portrait of Saunders differs dramatically from Catherine Goodman's painting in that it is a bronze head by Nigel Boonham. The material is of paramount importance here – dark in hue and highly textured, there is no use of colour to assist the likeness. It is not just the properties of metal that are significant, but the connotations of statues and their distinctive manner of display that need to be considered. Inevitably the associations with classical monuments come to viewers' minds, reinforced by the columnar stands on which sculpted heads are placed. The face is certainly recognisable from other portraits of Saunders; she is shown without spectacles and her hair is the most feminine feature. There are two distinct issues raised by such a portrait. The first is the status of sculpture in portraiture. Once a major form for the representation of significant figures, it is now associated primarily with public art, generally of a fairly conventional kind. The National Portrait Gallery currently commissions very few three-dimensional works compared with paintings and photographs, despite possessing some innovative works in a range of materials. Then there is the question of seeing a person in three dimensions rather than two. It might be thought that this would be more lifelike, but in practice the solidity of the material is seemingly at odds with the labile flesh it is meant to evoke.

These examples indicate that there are distinctive challenges in finding and deploying visual idioms that are apt for women subjects. But the material may pose challenges in representing men too. The College owns important three-dimensional portrayals of male sitters and, in interpreting them, gender differences are not the only consideration. Because there has been such a marked historical imbalance between men and women holding top posts, and the changes so slow, it is inevitable that, in looking at portraits of senior medical women, viewers register the fact of their femininity, which contrasts with longstanding masculine norms. Arguably it is artists not sitters who will find innovative ways of exploring and expressing gender.

Nigel Boonham, *Cicely Saunders*, 2001, bronze, 43cm high. © Nigel Boonham FRBS.

M.Chamberlain R.A. pinx.t

J. Collyer sculp.

Published as the Act directs by J. Collyer, 28 April 1783.

D.ʳ Wᵐ HUNTER, F.R.S.

To the Gentlemen of the Faculty, this Plate
Engraved from the Original Picture
in the Council Chamber of the Royal Academy,
is Inscribed by their
Obedᵗ Humᵇˡᵉ Servᵗ
J. Collyer.

Sold by J. Boydell Cheapside; W. Faden, Charing Cross & J. Collyer, White-Lion-Row, Islington.

INTIMACY AND DISTANCE

The foundational premise of portraiture is giving access to other human beings through the sense of sight, which might suggest a certain intimacy, first between artist and sitter and then between viewers and visual representations. In practice, the matter is not so straightforward. Evidence of the interactions between artists and their subjects may be elusive, although they are now being documented more fully by commissioning institutions such as the National Portrait Gallery. In some situations – Catherine Goodman painting the dying Cicely Saunders was one – intense closeness develops, while in others formality, distance and communication barriers exist, as was the case when Pietro Annigoni painted Moran (see pages 91–2).

The medium plays a crucial role in these relationships, as is evident if we compare the experience of looking at a small drawing, watercolour or miniature, with that of a large oil painting or a bust. Boonham's head of Cicely Saunders, for instance, is more than life size, and is displayed on a wooden stand, so that she is, more or less, at eye level. With small portraits the scale allows close inspection of an image that then appears informal and accessible. Grand manner paintings, by contrast, require the beholder to stand at a distance, while the hard materials used in sculpture – with their absence of flesh tones and the delicate textures of skin – prompt associations with public monuments and classical exemplars. When portraits have been designed to make statements about social status, professional success and the authority of the sitters, then intimacy is hardly the main issue. Viewers are expected to pick up on a range of visual cues and to interpret them in context, whether they do all this consciously or not. Portraits have been sufficiently ubiquitous, especially since the advent of print culture, to give large swathes of the population exposure to them; those who were not in a position to own portraits saw them in print shop windows, on coins and in the context of ephemera. Some levels of visual literacy were essential in everyday life.

More specific and sophisticated kinds of visual literacy were needed for those who made, bought and sold artefacts, whether these were two-dimensional images, books or objects such as jewellery, silver and glassware, ceramics and furniture. Collectors and connoisseurs, some of whom were medically trained, laid stress on their attentive-looking practices. More specifically, it is reasonable to assume honed forms of visual

OPPOSITE: Joseph Collyer after Mason Chamberlin, *William Hunter*, stipple, 1783, 18.2 x 11.2. While William Hunter was well connected with the royal family and the Royal Academy of Arts, for instance, he was a controversial figure, suspected of using grave robbers for his anatomy teaching. He holds an *écorché* figure, which shows the musculature under the skin. He died on 30 March 1783; this print was published less than a month later. Presumably his demise generated enough interest to justify another print.

ABOVE: Clive Riviere, *Clive Riviere*, 1925, 25.4 x 30.5.

literacy among medical professionals and those who commission portraits. Physicians draw upon a range of sensory experiences when learning their craft and making judgements about patients' health, among them the ability to perceive and interpret colour, shape, texture, demeanour and posture. It was commonplace well into the twentieth century for sketches to be made by those working with human tissues whether in the consulting room, hospital or laboratory. New digital technologies require fresh visual skills. In commissioning illustrations for textbooks, for instance, medical authors drew upon their visual habits and experiences, including skills acquired during training. Some practitioners were especially skilled, including those who were not artists themselves. William Hunter is a case in point, as the magnificent drawings and prints he organised for his book on the gravid uterus testify.[36]

Interestingly some medics were also artists. The College owns self-portraits by Henry Monro and by Clive Riviere, a distinguished chest physician and son of the well-known painter Briton Riviere. Some of the Monros displayed a strong commitment to the visual arts and the College possesses a number of portraits by family members. The self-portrait is a fine, sensitive study, probably painted when Henry Monro was in his early fifties. The portrait is elegant and somewhat formal; by contrast Clive Riviere's small, intense work shows him staring straight ahead and includes only his head and shoulders. His father and brother painted portraits, while there was both a doctor

ABOVE: Henry Monro, *Henry Monro*, c. 1870, 76.2 x 58.7.
Monro broke the family tradition of working at the Bethlem Hospital. He served as a physician to St Luke's Hospital for twenty-eight years and had a private practice. In 1857 he donated a number of family portraits to the College of which he had become a fellow in 1848. He presented this work in 1870.

Self-portraits bear direct testimony to the heightened visual engagement of their makers, and invite viewers to experience some immediate connection to the artist.

and an artist on his mother's side. Riviere's self-portrait is unusual in the context of the College's collection, but it may usefully be compared to the drawing that Henry Tonks, another doctor-artist, made of himself, probably around the same time. Tonks was a decade older than Riviere and a professional artist and art teacher, as well as a surgeon, who presented himself as an altogether more confident person. It is hard to say whether levels of skill play a part in the differences between these self-portraits. Nonetheless, self-portraits bear direct testimony to the heightened visual engagement of their makers, and invite viewers to experience some immediate connection to the artist.[37]

The College holds one portrait that excites particular interest and divides opinion, and I use it to probe the kinds of intimacy and distance that professional likenesses evoke. It reveals how portraits become entangled with reactions to sitters, which are strongly shaped by emotional and political factors, and by aesthetic responses to the artist's approach and style.

Pietro Annigoni spoke little English when he first visited the United Kingdom in 1949; over subsequent decades he painted many leading figures in British society, including HM Queen Elizabeth II in 1955. This portrait has become one of his most iconic works and adorns the cover of his 1977 autobiography.[38] In 1951 he painted one of the College's most controversial figures, Charles McMoran Wilson, who had become the first Baron Moran in 1943, having been knighted five years earlier. The contours of Moran's career are well known, including his success in building up the medical school at St Mary's Hospital, distinguished service in the First World War, his position as Churchill's doctor, close involvement with setting up the National Health Service and the publication of two works, *The Anatomy of Courage* in 1945 and *Churchill: The Struggle for Survival 1945–60* in 1966, fifteen months after its subject had died.[39] Much has been said about every aspect of his life and the mere mention of his name in medical circles can trigger strong reactions.

Moran's centrality in the medical life of twentieth-century Britain, as in that of the College over which he presided between 1941 and 1950, cannot be doubted. From his encounter with Annigoni resulted a truly remarkable work of art which, despite its small size, is arresting. The artist achieved a worldwide reputation, worked in fresco as well as oils and was also an accomplished sculptor. Douglas Black, President between 1977 and 1983, claimed that Annigoni's portrait of Moran 'captures precisely the masterly combination of strategy and tactics which enabled him to do so much'. The comment was made in the context of a biography of Moran, published in 1992, for which Black wrote the foreword, where he emphasises 'the strength of the idealism which inspired' its subject. This quality, he suggested, is not conveyed by the portrait.[40] Black's words illustrate one of the greatest difficulties in writing about portraiture, namely taking account of the complex prior commitments viewers bring with them. The sitter's nickname was 'Corkscrew Charlie' and it has been said, by those more critical of Moran, that his deviousness is apparent in Annigoni's work.

OPPOSITE: Henry Tonks, *Henry Tonks*, pencil on paper, 1900–1925, 36.6 x 26.2, National Portrait Gallery, London.

ABOVE: Pietro Annigoni, *Charles McMoran Wilson* (Lord Moran), 1951, 60.9 x 49.5.

Moran's father was a general practitioner. He became a fellow in 1921 and served as President for nine years. This work was commissioned by the College but not received until 1974, three years before the sitter's death. His published comments on the artist, written in the winter of 1953, are revealing:

'Scientific research begins with an idea. Then we go into our laboratories and test if it is true. Perhaps art is like that. Anyway, what interests me in Annigoni, apart from his art, is his subtle interpretation of human nature. You must have seen a bird pecking at the lawn, sharply looking up to see if there is danger, and then pecking again; that was how Annigoni painted my portrait. Down would go his head into the palette, and then up for a sharp concentrated gaze. After all, he had to paint a man he did not know, who was cut off from him by another tongue. I wondered, as I sat there, what he was doing, for there are always two alternatives open to the artist. He can reproduce mechanically feature by feature, until at length there is a glossy photographic likeness, and for this he would have authority. Plato told us that painting is an imitative art and that the pleasure we get from it is precisely in proportion to the faithfulness of the likeness. Or the artist can aim higher and try to tell you something about the sitter. One day I found that Annigoni was committed to the bolder plan. I had wanted to remonstrate with him over some touch of decay which he had introduced into the portrait, and with the help of a pocket dictionary I was grinding out my point, when he murmured: "It is an interpretation." Long ago Joshua Reynolds, in his discourses, said that a portrait that appeals only to the eye is just a likeness, but that a portrait that appeals to the imagination may be a work of art. Annigoni's portraits, by taking you into a man's life and telling you something about his past, seems to me to pass, triumphantly, Sir Joshua's test.'

The portrait itself provides the best point of departure. Annigoni was an exponent of an 'old master' approach to painting. The work in oils is highly finished and expresses a commitment to exactitude. The palette is dark and rich, with one side of the sitter's face highlighted. The pose is unusual, however, in that although Moran is shown seated in a chair holding a book and wearing robes, he is looking away from the viewer, whose eye is caught not just by one side of his face, but also by his left hand, with a ring on one finger. By virtue of the light coming from the spectator's right, his averted gaze and the slightly turned shoulders, the overall effect is of a twisted body. One interpretation is that Moran has been caught in a pensive mood by the artist with whom he is not engaging directly. Formal photographs of Moran show him with a similarly serious, even melancholy expression.[41]

In 1954 Moran wrote the foreword for a publication accompanying an exhibition in London of Annigoni's work, which included his own portrait. In his comments, quoted in the caption opposite, Moran likens the painter's approach to that of a scientist and insists on the high quality of his work, which goes beyond a mechanical likeness. It is a striking combination of claims, not least since Moran himself was not a laboratory scientist and he could easily have compared art to clinical practice. Charles Richard Cammell, the other contributor to the catalogue, was a poet who wrote extensively about art. He was complimentary about Moran's portrait and emphatic about the popularity of the exhibition at the Wildenstein Galleries in Bond Street.[42] In his autobiography, Annigoni relates his encounter not just with his sitter – 'the only opinion about him that I felt justified in forming … was that he was rather vain' – but with Lady Moran, through whom they communicated in French. Annigoni estimates that they had about forty sittings and mentions the frequency with which Moran made requests concerning the portrait, conveyed through notes scribbled by his wife.[43] It is unlikely that Moran would have been asked to write the foreword without the full approval of Annigoni. In his memoir, the artist mentioned his subject's connection with Churchill and the disapproval he incurred for publishing an account of his famous patient.

Such materials help build up an understanding of the contexts in which portraits are made, even if published reactions by sitters to those that paint them are relatively rare. Where commentary may find a resting place is in the portrait itself, which leads on to judgements about the kinds of skill artists exhibit, the traditions in which they work and their overall approach. In the case of those who have been critically acclaimed and extensively discussed, the evidence is considerably richer. Annigoni's aesthetic credo and worldwide fame are thus of central importance for any account of Moran's portrait.

Painting portraits is also a business that serves diverse markets, and is peopled by artists with a wide range of talents and skills, so it is hardly surprising that works of varying quality come into being. Since the goal is to capture something like the essence of a sitter, reactions to any given work are likely to diverge. At the same time, portraits play with viewers' reactions. On some occasions the scale and materials generate more or less predictable reactions. On others, the artist conceives a portrait in a fresh way, using an unexpected pose, as Annigoni did, producing a work that

Nigel Boonham, *Geoffrey Keynes*, bronze, 1976, 29.8 high.

gives the sitter a lively presence. It may not generate intimacy for most viewers, but it provides a strong sense that a human being has indeed been grasped and represented to viewers by the artist. Intimacy and distance are simultaneously involved in many interactions between portraits and beholders.

Moran was not himself a specialist in the visual arts, but as mentioned earlier some medical practitioners certainly were, and one such individual, a surgeon not a physician, is represented in the College's portrait collection. Geoffrey Keynes, a respected scholar and bibliophile as well as a medical practitioner, gave the Harveian Oration in 1958 and was subsequently elected a fellow of the College.[44] A decade later, he delivered the first Oslerian Oration at the College.[45] Keynes' passionate admiration for William Harvey, together with his deep interest in other medical figures, such as Thomas Browne, indicate the basis for his affinity with the College. Keynes not only enjoyed a long association with the National Portrait Gallery, but he was also on the fringes of the Bloomsbury group, mixing with writers and artists. Nigel Boonham, who sculpted him, credits Keynes with encouraging him to undertake portraits. Given the generation to which he belonged, there are many photographs of Keynes, including a fine one, signed and dated by both him and the Cambridge studio Ramsay and Muspratt, where it was taken.[46] The drawing of him by Stanley Spencer is of special interest. At this point sitter and artist had known each other for more than forty years. It came into the Portrait Gallery's collections in 2010, following the death of Milo, Geoffrey's third son, a surgeon and author with an interest in portraits, like his father. Milo had inherited the Spencer drawing in 1982 following Geoffrey's death. In correspondence concerning his bequest, Milo revealed that his mother and brothers did not *like* the drawing.[47]

'Liking' portraits or not, as the case may be, is a tricky but unavoidable matter. It may express a reaction to the manner in which the artist works, it could signal a discrepancy between the viewer's sense of the subject and the image before them, or a combination of the two. 'Like' is hard to analyse, yet it is probably the most common notion invoked in everyday interactions with portraits. Furthermore people feel entitled to voice such views, regardless of whether they know the sitter personally or not, or indeed anything about the picture. When the College asks fellows to contribute to the not inconsiderable cost of commissioning a portrait, the fellows acquire, as it were, a further stake in the end result. Few of them write to the College to share their reactions, but there is sufficient correspondence in the archives to reveal the strength of feeling about portraits from many periods. 'Liking' is a personal reaction and beneath it lies the tangled

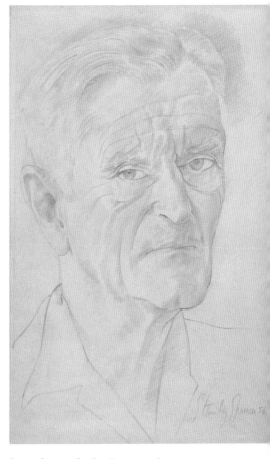

Stanley Spencer, *Geoffrey Keynes*, pencil on paper, 1956, 40.2 x 26. National Portrait Gallery, London.

ways in which a portrait of one person touches another. Professional situations, no less than personal ones, elicit these complexities, and in interpreting the College's collection such feelings need to be acknowledged. Person-to-portrait responses involve all the maelstrom of emotions familiar from daily life, where prejudice and insecurities as well as gender, age, appearance, expression and much more come into play.

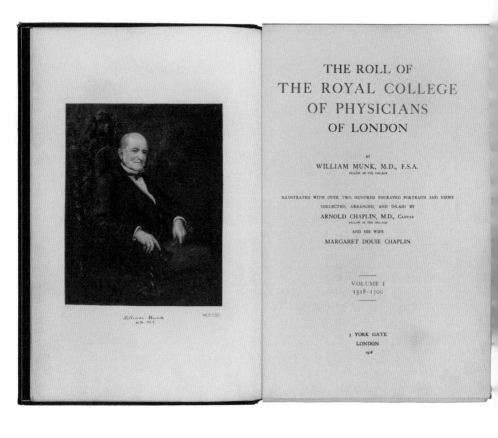

ABOVE: Arnold Chaplin and Margaret Douie Chaplin, *The Roll of the Royal College of Physicians of London by William Munk*, 1918, prints, photographs and printed text, bound volumes 52.7 x 35.5, pages are a little smaller.

PORTRAITS AS SOLACE

One of the most remarkable items in the College's collections is an extra-illustrated version of Munk's *Roll*. Using the second edition, published in 1878, Arnold Chaplin and his wife, Margaret Douie Chaplin, worked together to insert portrait prints of key figures into three large volumes. This idea of breaking up a published book and remaking it by linking its text with prints became fashionable in the eighteenth century and is also known as 'Grangerisation' after James Granger's 1769 publication, *A Biographical History of England*. Granger set out a system for arranging portrait collections, although the practice of extra-illustration is known to precede his book by several decades.[48] Using prints in a variety of ways, including sticking them up on walls, was a type of recreation. In medical contexts it articulated an affinity with past figures who had practised the same occupation. It is vital to stress the painstaking work required to fit both prints and book pages into their mounts.

There is ample evidence of portrait prints being part of collecting practices, for example by Anthony Askew and William Osler, who, in addition to the portraits used as frontispieces in his vast library, owned an extra-illustrated version of *The Gold-headed Cane*. This work is listed in *Bibliotheca Osleriana*, which indicates that its possible provenance was noted in Osler's hand inside the volume. The creator had used Munk's edition of 1884, which contained additional lives of Halford, Paris and Mayo, and had inserted 110 illustrations.[49]

Prints came in many formats and used a range of techniques; they could be cheap, and hence accessible, while large fine prints, such as the mezzotints in the Chaplins' volume, carried more prestige and a higher price tag.[50] Extra-illustrated works varied in terms of size, sophistication, the print techniques represented and the cost of the images, and thus could be adapted to suit a variety of incomes and tastes. The Chaplins' project provides unusually direct evidence of the significance of portraits in medical contexts.

Arnold Chaplin was a chest physician with wide interests, including in French and English history. In 1913 he published a book on Napoleon's last illness and death. He had become a fellow of the College in 1902, married seven years later, and in 1918 was appointed Harveian Librarian. The extra-illustrated volumes are dated 1918 and most of the prints are portraits. Also in the College's collections are loose prints bearing Chaplin's name. Thus he was a sufficiently dedicated and enthusiastic collector to have enough for the three volumes by William Munk – which contain over two hundred prints, forty-four of which depict buildings with medical associations – and some to spare, although these may have been acquired after the extra-illustration project was completed.

Preface

We have now completed the work of Extra-Illustrating "The Roll of the Royal College of Physicians of London" by William Munk, M.D. F.R.C.P. F.S.A, and it is fitting that we should give some account of the undertaking. The task now accomplished has been entirely a labour of love. We have spent many hours of happy leisure in mounting the Portraits and sheets of the "letter-press." We have laid under contribution most of the Printsellers of London and elsewhere in our search for Portraits and other Illustrations for the purpose of this work. Often, great has been our joy when, after much labour, some scarcely hoped-for Portrait has been secured.

We do not pretend that our "Inlaying of Portraits" is equal to the work of professional "Inlayers"; but we decided from the first that the book should be entirely "Extra-Illustrated" by our own hands, and that we would throw into the task all our energy, and whatever little skill we might possess or acquire. During the long black period of the War, we have laboured at this book, and as it engrossed our attention more and more, and grew under our hands, we came to regard it as a solace, and a sure remedy for the sadness occasioned by that terrible cataclysm.

While working we have been in the habit of associating ourselves, in the spirit, with the men whose Biographies and Portraits are contained in the work. We have formed our likes, and our dislikes, We have speculated on their characters, and we have often felt as if we were living in their time, and were sharing their joys and sorrows. With the Portraits and Biographies before us we seemed to possess a clearer perception of the characters of the men to whom they belong.

Some seventeen hundred names appear on the College Roll, from the date of incorporation to the year 1825. Of these, the Portraits of some two hundred are known to have been engraved, and perhaps another hundred and fifty Portraits are in existence which have never been the subject of the Engraver's art. Doubtless also, a search amongst family collections of Pictures would reveal many more the existence of which was unknown. Except in a few instances, we have confined our collection of Portraits to those which have been engraved, and we have left blank sheets with the hope that omissions will, some day, be rectified.

The book is now finished, and we have for it a great affection, not only on account of the honest work we have bestowed upon it, but also, because of the memories of happy companionship it recalls. For us it will always be a memorial of our close association. When, however, the time has come that we are no more, we hope the Royal College of Physicians of London will see fit to accept these three volumes as evidence of our respect for that ancient and honourable body.

Arnold Chaplin

3 York Gate. N.W.
January 9th 1918.

Margaret D. Chaplin

The handwritten preface sets out how the couple approached their work in the context of wartime and the comfort they found in it. Portraits of each of them follow this explanatory note, which was signed by them both. Their preface movingly expresses many of the sentiments that portraits elicit. The work was undertaken during 'many hours of happy leisure'. Yet it involved considerable labour, they stress, not least in tracking down the prints they wanted. It is entirely their own work, even if it is not as accomplished as that of professional 'Inlayers'. They continue:

'while working we have been in the habit of associating ourselves, in the spirit, with the men whose Biographies and Portraits are contained in the work. We have formed our likes and our dislikes. … we have often felt as if we were living in their time, and were sharing their joys and sorrows.'

OPPOSITE: The handwritten preface.
ABOVE: An opening from the Chaplins' work.

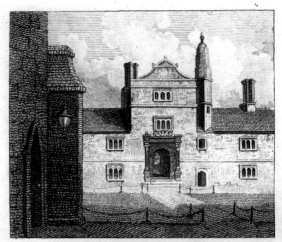

CAIUS COLLEGE

JOHN CAIUS M.D.

Artist and engraver unknown, *John Caius*, stipple, 1801, 19.2 x 10.75.
This print, showing the Cambridge College with which Caius' name is associated, was published by Edward Harding, librarian to Queen Charlotte. While not a founding father, Caius, who served as President several times between 1555 and 1571, and enjoyed royal appointments, was a distinguished scholar who added lustre to the College's history.

This is eloquent testimony of the power of portraits, of a distinctive type of historical imagination and of the personal responses the combination of biography and portraiture provokes.

Well-known names from the College's history are there, starting with Henry VIII, Linacre and Caius, through to Thomas Young, Thomas Southwood Smith and James McGrigor. They also included portraits of men trained in medicine but who are better known for their non-medical activities, such as Charles Meryon, who wrote about Lady Hester Stanhope's travels; John Good, an exceptional linguist who was a translator and literary man, as well as a practising physician; and Charles Daubeny, the geologist and mineralogist.

Other themes run through the preface: love and affection, solace, work as a remedy for sadness. Their words express their affection for each other as well as for the book they created; these are intermingled with a sense of the effort and attention the task required, and with their respect for the College – 'that ancient and venerable body'. Above all, it was a labour of love.

TOP RIGHT: William Miller, after an unknown artist, *Thomas Linacre*, 1810, 48.3 x 36.8.
Linacre holds a special place as a founding father and the first President of the College, a post he held for six years. A learned physician with royal connections, Linacre could be said to have inaugurated a model of professional success emulated by many of his successors. In later life he combined physic with the priesthood.
BOTTOM RIGHT: George Richmond after Hans Holbein, *William Butts*, 1880, 47 x 38.1.
Butts was an early fellow of the College and treated Henry VIII. This copy was made in the Victorian period by a successful, well-connected portrait painter; it shows how highly valued likenesses of early fellows were. That the original was by Holbein was also an attractive feature.

Margaret D. Chaplin

Arnold Chaplin.

ABOVE: Photographers unknown, Margaret Douie Chaplin and Arnold Chaplin, 1918, photographs.

CONCLUDING COMMENTS: LABOURS OF LOVE

'Love' is not too strong a word to express at least some of the sentiments surrounding portraits; it was used unselfconsciously by Arnold and Margaret Chaplin of their project to extra-illustrate Munk's biographies. Geoffrey Keynes admitted he 'hero-worshipped' Harvey, while Osler's collecting practices expressed his deep affinity with Thomas Browne, whom he thought of as his 'life-long mentor'.[51] Osler himself inspired great affection and veneration. Richard Mead and William Hunter owned portraits of William Harvey, because he was an inspiration for them. The College has been the focal point for five hundred years of many such heartfelt associations, which portraits express. Likenesses hold associations between people, who keep affinities fresh through social practices, such as dinners and speeches, and through more personal ones, such as reading, collecting and looking. A major collector in its own right, the College has benefited from the collections of others, both medical and lay. Inevitably, it has been the location of rows, tensions and rifts, jealousies and rivalries, as well as of friendship and patronage. Reactions to the portrait of Moran hint at some of the strong personal responses and political difficulties that occur in any institution, and that portraits cannot escape. Writing about such a portrait collection is to walk a tightrope. It is necessary to find a balance between personal reactions, assessments of quality, providing context, conveying the diversity of the collection and revealing its significance. The centrality of portraits in British public life is not in doubt. Nor is the complexity of the genre, which its promise of revealing what another person looked like, belies. Portraits, through the visual intelligence of their makers, work to prompt remembrance, affirm status, confer honour, express gratitude and above all to give a special kind of life to those who make institutions possible.

Reactions to the portrait of Moran hint at some of the strong personal responses and political difficulties that occur in any institution, and that portraits cannot escape. Writing about such a portrait collection is to walk a tightrope.

ENDNOTES

1   Barnabas Calder, *Denys Lasdun's Royal College of Physicians. A Monumental Act of Faith*, London, 2008, e.g. pp. 15 and 41; Rowan Moore, *Anatomy of a Building*, London, 2014; Lord Platt, *Private and Controversial*, London, 1972, p. 109.

2   John Harley Warner addresses this as well as other themes that run through this book from an American perspective in 'The Aesthetic Grounding of Modern Medicine', *Bulletin of the History of Medicine*, 88, 2014, 1–47. Both William Osler and Luke Fildes' *The Doctor* feature in his account.

3   Christopher Lawrence and Steven Shapin, eds, *Science Incarnate: Historical Embodiments of Natural Knowledge*, Chicago and London, 1998, especially Chapter 5 by Christopher Lawrence, 'Medical Minds, Surgical Bodies: Corporeality and the Doctors', pp. 156–201.

4   William Rubin, *Picasso and Portraiture: Representation and Transformation*, London, 1996; on portraiture more generally, see Richard Brilliant, *Portraiture*, London, 1991; Joanna Woodall, ed., *Portraiture: Facing the Subject*, Manchester, 1997; Shearer West, *Portraiture*, Oxford, 2004.

5   Alastair Smart, *Allan Ramsay: A Complete Catalogue of his Paintings*, New Haven and London, 1999, pp. 157–8.

6   Malcolm Baker and David Bindman, *Roubiliac and the Eighteenth-century Monument*, New Haven and London, 1995, on Mead, pp. 21 and 241.

7   David Mannings, *Sir Joshua Reynolds. A Complete Catalogue of his Paintings*, two volumes, New Haven and London, 2000; for William Pitcairn and Charles Lucas, see text volume, pp. 377 and 312. Martin Postle, ed., *Joshua Reynolds: The Creation of Celebrity*, London, 2005.

8   Boonham's website (www.boonham.com) contains material on his contact with Geoffrey Keynes. The College's archives contain comments he made about sculpting Saunders.

9   Geoffrey Keynes, *The Life of William Harvey*, Oxford, 1966, and *The Gates of Memory*, Oxford, 1983, Chapter 24, concern his work on Harvey and at the National Portrait Gallery. A recent popular biography of Harvey is Thomas Wright, *Circulation: William Harvey's Revolutionary Idea*, London, 2012.

10 A recent example is David Wootton, *The Invention of Science: A New History of the Scientific Revolution*, London, 2015.

11 There are many editions of Harvey's work, for example: William Harvey, *The Circulation of the Blood and Other Writings* (translated by Kenneth J. Franklin), London, 1963.

12 Geoffrey Keynes, *The Portraiture of William Harvey*, London, 1949.

13 The book exists in many versions, listed on pp. 25–6 of the edition published by the College in 1968 to mark its 450th anniversary: William Macmichael, *The Gold-headed Cane. A Facsimile of the Author's 1827 Copy...*, London, 1968. In his Preface, Max Rosenheim called the cane 'a symbol of culture and art in medical practice' (p.iii).

14 Munk's edition was not illustrated.

15   The roles of royal physicians in England remain an under-explored field, but see Vivian Nutton, ed., *Medicine at the Courts of Europe*, London, 1990 and especially the chapter by W. F. Bynum.

16   George York and David Steinberg, *Introduction to the Life and Work of John Hughlings Jackson with a catalogue raisonné of his writings*, London, 2006 (*Medical History* supplement no. 26).

17   Robert Willan LRCP 1785 (https://artuk.org/discover/artworks/robert-willan-17571812-192319). Franco Crainz, *The Life and Works of Matthew Baillie M.D. ...*, 1995, no place of publication given. This labour of love uses Baillie's manuscript autobiography; it includes many portraits and a section on his famous patients in a classic instance of elevation by association.

18   There is now considerable discussion over the nature of celebrity; its association with portraiture is usefully explored in Postle, ed., *Joshua Reynolds,* op. cit.

19   Ludmilla Jordanova, 'Science, Memory and Relics in Britain', in Marco Beretta, Maria Conforti and Paolo Mazzarello, eds, *Savant Relics: Brains and Remains of Scientists*, Sagamore Beach, MA, 2016, pp. 157–181, which uses a number of medical examples.

20   Maude Abbott, ed., *The Sir William Osler Memorial Volume*, Montreal, 1926 is a huge tome which, published a mere seven years after his death and extensively illustrated, gives a strong sense of the importance of souvenirs. Alex Sakula, *The Portraiture of Sir William Osler*, London and New York, 1991, p. 32 mentions an American doctor who owned a portrait of him, 'collected other Osler memorabilia, including Osler's overcoat, a chair and a pair of bookends'.

21   Earl Nation, Charles Roland and John McGovern, eds, *An Annotated Checklist of Osleriana*, Kent, Ohio, 1976, p. vii. The very term 'Osleriana' suggests nostalgia-tinged celebration of and curiosity about everything to do with Osler. For a recent and thoroughly historical take on Osler, see Michael Bliss, *William Osler: A Life in Medicine*, New York, 1999, especially the last chapter on his afterlife.

22   *A Catalogue ... to which is added the Collection of Prints and Drawings of Dr. Anthony Askew, deceased*, London, 1775, pp. 84–5, many of the entries are groups of portrait prints, e.g. numbers 5–11, 23, 26 and 42–3. I consulted the copy in Cambridge University Library. *Bibliotheca Askeviana sive catalogus Librorum Rarissimorum Antonii Askew...*, London, 1775. This is a complex list, organised by day of sale, size of book and language. For Harvey's *Opera*, see p. 63; Celsus's *De Medicina*, p. 52. Askew also owned works by Garth and Mead, the 1715 *Life of Dr. Radcliffe*, a history of the Royal Society, books by Newton and much more, especially editions of the classics. He also owned the sales catalogues for Freind's library and Mead's collections. I consulted the copy in Emmanuel College Library and Archives, which also owns his *Liber Amicorum* kept when he was travelling in 1746 and 1747, and includes an inscription by Albrecht von Haller, the great German doctor.

23   These are the figures from the College who feature in his Bibliotheca Prima: William Osler, *Bibliotheca Osleriana: a Catalogue of Books illustrating the History of Medicine and Science...*, Montreal and London, 1969. This was first published in 1929, ten years after Osler's death. He was working on it when he died. On page xvi, the editors quote Osler's thoughts on designating a few works as Bibliotheca Prima: '... the idea is to have in a comparatively small number of works the essential literature grouped about the men of the first rank...'.

24   Smart, *Allan Ramsay*, op. cit., p. 74.

25   James Wardrop, *The Works of Matthew Baillie M.D., to which is prefixed an account of his life, collected from authentic sources*, two volumes, London, 1825. The quotations come from volume I, pp. viii and xlvi.

26   Thomas Young died in 1829 before the term 'scientist' was in common use. Indeed many nineteenth-century figures we now think of in this way disliked the term, see Ruth Barton, '"Men of Science": Language, Identity and Professionalization in the Mid-Victorian Scientific Community', *History of Science*, xli, 2003, pp. 73–119. On his portrait by Lawrence see Kenneth Garlick, *Sir Thomas Lawrence. A Complete Catalogue of the Oil Paintings*, Oxford, 1989, p. 290.

27   Anne Digby, *Making a Medical Living: Doctors and their Patients in the English Market for Medicine, 1720–1911*, Cambridge, 1994, especially Chapter 6 on Physicians, and her closing reflections.

28   W. F. Bynum and Caroline Overy, eds, *Michael Foster and Thomas Henry Huxley: Correspondence, 1865–1895*, London, 2009 (*Medical History* supplement no. 28).

29   Jordanova, '… Relics…', pp. 166–71, especially p. 168 on claims about Harvey, science and experiment, op. cit.

30   Marie Boas Hall, *All Scientists Now: The Royal Society in the Nineteenth Century*, Cambridge, 1984.

31   L. V. Fildes, *Luke Fildes R.A.: A Victorian Painter*, London 1968, p. 46. The precise identity of 'Dr Murray' remains unclear; see p. 120 on doctors whom Fildes knew being keen to sit for the picture, including Thomas Buzzard (FRCP 1873), but it 'was not a portrait of any one individual; it was a composite out of the painter's imagination', and p. 123 on the success of the picture, including as print and postage stamp, in the United States.

32   Richard Ormond and Elaine Kilmurray, *John Singer Sargent: the Later Portraits*, New Haven and London, 2003, pp. 38–9. Sargent also painted Silas Weir Mitchell in 1903 (pp. 112–3) and Osler along with three other doctors in 1905–6 (pp.149–52).

33   There is material on Vaughan in the registered packet in the National Portrait Gallery archive (NPG 5928). See also Geoffrey Davenport, Ian McDonald and Caroline Moss-Gibbons, eds, *The Royal College of Physicians and its Collections: An Illustrated History*, London, 2001, pp. 36–39, 'Women's Place in the College', especially p. 39.

34   I am drawing here on the record of a conversation between her and a member of the College's staff about the commission, which is in the Archives.

35   An indication of her reputation is her inclusion in Gordon Brown's book, *Courage: Eight Portraits*, London, 2007, Chapter 7. Chapter 1 concerns the nurse Edith Cavell.

36   William Hunter, *Anatomia Uteri Humani Gravidi Tabulis Illustrata*, London, 1774. On William Hunter there is W. F. Bynum and Roy Porter, eds, *William Hunter and the Eighteenth-century Medical World*, Cambridge, 1985, and Peter Black, ed., *My Highest Pleasures: William Hunter's Art Collection*, London, 2007.

37   Self-portraits have been an object of interest for many centuries, precisely because they appear to promise direct access to artists' inner lives. In practice, artists construct the image they wish to project. A recent account is James Hall, *The Self-Portrait: A Cultural History*, London, 2014. On Tonks there is Joseph Hone, *The Life of Henry Tonks*, London, 1939. See also Suzannah Biernoff, *Portraits of Violence: War and the Aesthetics of Disfigurement*, Ann Arbor, 2017 which discusses Tonks' portraits of injured soldiers.

38   Pietro Annigoni, *An Artist's Life. As told to Robert Wraight*, London, 1977; Charles Richard Cammell, *Memoirs of Annigoni*, London, 1956, p. 98 refers to Moran; *Museo Pietro Annigoni Villa Bardini Firenze*, Livorno, 2009.

39   Lord Moran, *The Anatomy of Courage. The Classic WWI Account of the Psychological Effects of War*, London 2007, first published, 1945; *Churchill: The Struggle for Survival 1940–65: taken from the Diaries of Lord Moran*, London, 1968, first published in 1966 and available in several editions.

40   Black in Richard Lovell, *Churchill's Doctor. A Biography of Lord Moran*, London and New York, 1992, p.vii.

41   Three photographs on the National Portrait Gallery website illustrate the point: NPG x23813, x23819 and x95271. In two he rests his head on his hand, a pose sometimes associated with melancholy and also with learned men seated by a table.

42   There are two versions and two editions of the catalogue, the ones in Cambridge University Library in a larger format (31 cm) contain the Moran Preface: *Pietro Annigoni with an Introduction by Charles Richard Cammell; and a foreword by Lord Moran*, London 1954. A second revised edition appeared in 1958.

43   Annigoni, *Artist's Life*, op. cit., pp. 74–6, quotation on p. 74.

44   Keynes, *Gates,* op. cit., p. 307.

45   This is reprinted in his autobiography, *Gates*, pp. 392–410.

46   NPG x1091, where there is also a version of the Boonham bust, NPG 5182.

47   Keynes, *Gates*, op. cit., p. 117. Other information is from the Registered Packet for the Spencer drawing, NPG 6890.

48   Marcia Pointon, *Hanging the Head: Portraiture and Social Formation in Eighteenth-century England*, New Haven and London, 1993, pp. 53–78 on Granger and Grangerisation; the website of the Ashmolean Museum, Oxford contains a useful introduction to extra-illustration: http://sutherland.ashmolean.museum/Grangerization.shtml. Also, Lucy Peltz, *Facing the Text: Extra-illustration, Print Culture, and Society in Britain*, 1769–1840, San Marino CA, 2017 is the most authoritative account.

49   Osler, *Bibliotheca*, 1969, op. cit., no. 6720, p. 576.

50   Anthony Griffiths, *Prints and Printmaking: an Introduction to the History and Techniques*, 2nd edition, London, 1996.

51   Osler, *Bibliotheca,* op. cit., p. xvi, the editors quoting Osler.

SELECT BIBLIOGRAPHY

Barton, Ruth, 'Men of Science': Language, Identity and Professionalization in the Mid-Victorian Scientific Community', *History of Science*, 2003, 41, 73–119.

Bliss, Michael, *William Osler: A Life in Medicine*, New York, 1999.

Brain, Lord, *Doctors Past and Present*, London, 1964.

Bynum, W. F. and Caroline Overy, eds, *Michael Foster and Thomas Henry Huxley: Correspondence, 1865–1895*, London, 2009 (*Medical History* Supplement no 28).

Craintz, F., *The Life and Works of Matthew Baillie M.D....*, London, 1990.

Cushing, Harvey, *The Life of William Osler*, Oxford, 1925.

Davenport, Geoffrey et al, eds, *The Royal College of Physicians and its Collections: An Illustrated History*, London, 2001.

Digby, Anne, *Making a Medical Living: Doctors and their Patients in the English Market for Medicine, 1720–1911*, Cambridge, 1994.

Driver, A. H., *Catalogue of Engraved Portraits in the Royal College of Physicians of London*, London, 1952.

Griffiths, Anthony, *Prints and Printmaking: An Introduction to the History and Techniques*, 2nd edition, London, 1996.

Gunther, A. E., *An Introduction to the Life of the Rev. Thomas Birch D.D. F.R.S. 1705–1766*, Halesworth, 1984.

Hall, Marie Boas, *All Scientists Now: The Royal Society in the Nineteenth Century*, Cambridge, 1984.

Hancock, E. Geoffrey, Nick Pearce and Mungo Campbell, eds, *William Hunter's World: the Art and Science of Eighteenth-century Collecting*, Farnham, Surrey, 2015.

Hanson, Craig, *The English Virtuoso: Art, Medicine and Antiquarianism in the Age of Empiricism*, Chicago and London, 2009.

Hone, Joseph, *The Life of Henry Tonks*, London, 1939.

Jordanova, Ludmilla, *The Sense of a Past in Eighteenth-century Medicine*, Reading, 1997.

Jordanova, Ludmilla, 'Portraits, People and Things: Richard Mead and Medical Identity', *History of Science*, 61, 2003, 293–313.

Jordanova, Ludmilla, *Defining Features: Scientific and Medical Portraits, 1660–2000*, London, 2000.

Jordanova, Ludmilla, 'Science, Memory and Relics in Britain' in Marco Beretta, Maria Conforti and Paolo Mazzarello, eds, *Savant Relics: Brains and Remains of Scientists*, Sagamore Beach, MA, 2016, 157–181.

Keynes, Geoffrey, *The Life of Harvey*, Oxford, 1966.

Keynes, Geoffrey, *The Portraiture of William Harvey*, London, 1949 (The Thomas Vicary Lecture, 1948).

Keynes, Geoffrey, *The Gates of Memory*, Oxford and New York, 1983.

Lawrence, Christopher and Steven Shapin, eds, *Science Incarnate: Historical Embodiments of Natural Knowledge*, Chicago and London, 1998.

Lovell, Richard, *Churchill's Doctor. A Biography of Lord Moran*, London and New York, 1992.

[Macmichael, William], *The Gold-headed Cane*, London, 1827.

Moran, Lord, *The Anatomy of Courage*, London 2007 (first published 1945).

Moran, Lord, *Churchill: The Struggle for Survival 1940–60: taken from the Diaries of Lord Moran*, London, 1966.

Munk, William, *The Life of Sir Henry Halford*, London, 1895.

Munk, William, *The Roll of the Royal College of Physicians of London*, 2 volumes, London, 1861 and 2nd edition, 3 volumes, 1878.

Nutton, Vivien, ed., *Medicine at the Courts of Europe*, London, 1990.

Osler, William, *Bibliotheca Osleriana*, new edition, Montreal and London, 1969 (edited by W. W. Francis, R. H. Hill and Archibald Malloch).

Platt, Lord, *Private and Controversial*, London, 1972.

Pettigrew, William, *Medical Portrait Gallery*, 4 volumes, London, 1838–40.

Sakula, Alex, *The Portraiture of Sir William Osler*, London and New York, 1991.

Simon, Jacob, *The Art of the Picture Frame: Artists, Patrons and the Framing of Portraits in Britain*, London, 1996.

Solkin, David, *Art in Britain 1660–1815*, New Haven, 2015.

Stubbings, Frank, 'Anthony Askew's *Liber Amicorum*', *Transactions of the Cambridge Bibliographical Society*, 1972–6, 4, 306–321.

Turner-Warwick, Margaret, *Living Medicine: Recollections and Reflections*, London, 2005.

Warner, John Harley, 'in 'The Aesthetic Grounding of Modern Medicine', *Bulletin of the History of Medicine*, 88, 2014, 1–47.

Wilson, Charles McMoran, *see* Moran.

Wilton, Andrew, *The Swagger Portrait: Grand Manner Portraiture in Britain from Van Dyck to Augustus John*, London, 1992.

Wolstenholme, Gordon, ed., *The Royal College of Physicians of London: Portraits*, London, 1964.

Wolstenholme, Gordon and John Kerslake, *The Royal College of Physicians of London, Portraits Catalogue 2*, London, 1977.

Woodall, Joanne, ed. *Portraiture: Facing the Subject*, Manchester, 1997.

INDEX OF NAMES AND INSTITUTIONS